It gives me great pleasure . . . .

...It Gives Me

Great Pleasure...

BY

EMILY KIMBROUGH

ILLUSTRATED BY

Helen Hokinson

Dodd, Mead & Company • New York

The chapters titled *It Gives Me Great Pleasure* . . .; *A Railway Station, Every Time*; *Luggage for the South*; *"Cincinati and I"*; *Love—On a Train*; *In a Manner of Speaking* and *It's the Hospitality*, originally appeared in somewhat different form as stories in *The New Yorker*.

DESIGNED BY STEFAN SALTER

PRINTED IN THE UNITED STATES OF AMERICA
BY THE CORNWALL PRESS, INC., CORNWALL, N. Y.

To Sophia Yarnall Jacobs
with love and gratitude

Contents

Contents

It Gives Me Great Pleasure . . . .

"*Ladies, I know how disappointed all of us were not to have General Romulo with us this afternoon . . .*"

"IT GIVES ME great pleasure," says the program chairman, and she and I know that she is, like a croquet player, up to the last two wickets. The audience must know, too, that she is approaching the stake because there have been few introductions on any platform that did not wind up with, "and so it gives me great pleasure to present——" But this is the point at which only the chairman and I, from past experience, share an anxiety. Sometimes I am standing in the wings waiting to hear myself introduced; frequently I am in a chair behind her. Wherever I am, my toes are curled with anxiety, and from the way she shifts her position at this point, I have a conviction that hers are too. Will she accomplish the who I am and what I am?

A club president introducing my friend Helen Howe for a program of monologues, caused that artist some anxiety. Miss Howe is the distinguished daughter of the distinguished Mark Antony DeWolfe Howe. The club president, however, in an erratic carom shot, rendered it:

"It gives me great pleasure to introduce the distinguished daughter of the distinguished Mark Antony DeWolfe Hopper, winner himself of the Pulsifer Prize for writing the Barrett Wendell Letters," and then she hit the stake. "Miss Helen Howe," she concluded with a triumphant dip in the direction of the astonished Miss Howe.

A president in Minnesota shot through to me, however, with disconcerting accuracy.

"Ladies," she said, "I know how disappointed all of us were not to have General Romulo with us this afternoon, and so afraid that we would not have a program at all, we would have been glad of anybody. It therefore gives me great pleasure to introduce Miss Emily Kimbrough."

A chairman in Wisconsin, too, approached me with a forthright aim that made me flinch.

"Ladies, I apologize to you for our last program. I have no hesitancy in saying that it was so poor, I consider it a disaster. We hope that our speaker this afternoon will help us to forget that previous selection, and so it gives me great pleasure to present Miss Emily Kimbrough." Miss Kimbrough's knees were buckling as she approached the lectern.

But the program chairman in Texas never got through to me at all and small wonder. She was harried out of position once too often.

We came on the stage together, I marching a few paces behind her, as she had instructed when we waited in the wings for the audience to settle. She carried a black leather note book, a book on parliamentary rules, bound in red, and a small pale blue handkerchief. She confided in a whisper that she never carried a pocketbook because it was too hard to handle, and made her nervous. At the center of the stage, she stopped behind a lectern, placed her books and handkerchief on it, and bowed me to a high-backed chair upholstered in green velvet, and placed behind and a little to her left. It was one in a row of empty chairs spreading across the stage almost to the wings on either side, but it was the only one done in green velvet. I wondered who was coming to fill the empty seats. The chairman tapped the desk lightly with her gavel.

"Ladies," she began, but got no further. An usher was standing in one of the aisles, below the stage, waving a note up to her. I could see that, apart from the nervous strain of the interruption, the chairman was suffering a trembling involvment of her bifocals as she adjusted her vision to the usher and the waving note. I think she was flustered, too, at having to stoop down and bend over the footlights to take the note, because that necessitated holding onto her hat with one hand. Obviously, a new permanent had pushed it higher and more insecurely on her head than its accustomed position. It was a jaunty hat, of bright flowers and a ribbon bow, but it wobbled.

She brought back the note to the lectern and, before reading it aloud, made a few experimental tries to get it exactly the right distance away from her and under the small reading lamp clipped to the outer edge of the lectern. The message, itself, caused a considerable flurry in the audience. One of the members, it said, had parked her car at an angle more acute than that of the other cars and another member swinging into place beside it, had dented the fender. The offender stated her

honorable intentions of making amends, request-
ing only the name of the owner, and she gave the
license number. There was an agitated snapping
of pocketbooks, and general fumbling, while the
members of the audience extracted their owners'
cards to ascertain their license numbers. A small
blond woman, whose hat was flowered and rib-
boned too, rose to her feet, waving a card at the
chairman on the platform.

"It's my car," she said, "I knew I wasn't
parked very well, but I tried twice and I thought
I wouldn't get a good seat if I tried again . . .
people were coming in so fast. I just can't seem
to park when I have to go in at an angle."

There were murmurs of sympathetic understanding throughout the audience. The writer of
the note rose up in one of the back rows, identify-
ing herself. It had all been her fault, she declared,
she should never have tried to get into that space.
She was as sorry as she could be. She didn't believe though that the dent would ever show after
it was fixed. The victim of the accident said she
was sure it wouldn't. She and the culprit bobbed
heads at each other to show that there was no
hard feeling between them and they both sat
down.

The audience required a moment or two in which to express its satisfaction with the exchange, before returning their attention to the platform. Then we were off again.

"Ladies," the chairman gathered them all in sternly for a second start. This was, she told them, the opening meeting of the season. The older members placed in the front row in order to hear, smiled complacently and nodded to corroborate her statement. She bowed suddenly to a generously proportioned lady whom I had not noticed until this official recognition. The lady was at a piano below the stage, to the right of us, regarding the chairman with the tension of a runner awaiting the pistol shot, and at the nod, she set off immediately with a loud chord.

I had been, until this moment, only an interested and relaxed spectator. The chord, however, was like a pistol shot to me too, and I leaped to my feet. From past experience, I surmised that it prefaced a community rendering of the National Anthem. I was mistaken, but for the moment before I perceived my error, I had an excellent view of the back of the hall, and two young girl ushers there, dressed in white, and wearing, in addition, a broad green satin ribbon

8

across the shoulder and fastened at the hip. They knew the meaning of the chord better than I. At the instant I arose, they opened wide the folding doors at the back of the hall, to disclose a line of women standing there, waiting.

One of the ushers called, "Ready!" The pianist resolved the chord miraculously into Pomp and Circumstance; the chairman called out high and clear, "Our Past Presidents," and single file, a procession advanced up the room. The presidents varied in age, size, and shape, but each one wore diagonally across her bosom, a wide green satin ribbon, fastened at the hip. Some of the bosoms were substantial, others meagre, and each bore, in addition to the ribbon band, a magnificent orchid. The presidents evidenced a regal indifference to keeping time, and so the line moved more erratically than most parades.

My musical confusion caused the only infringement upon the solemnity of the moment. Some of the audience interpreted my rising as a tribute to the marching leaders, and stood up too. Others did not. The front row was displeased, because, turning in their seats to anticipate the approach of the presidents, they found their view obstructed by those members who were standing.

9

Even the past presidents, themselves, were deflected from their individual rhythms by the risings and sittings along each row, and the line wavered indecisively. The chairman seemed to sense that I had something to do with all this, and she dealt with me efficiently. Turning round halfway, to include me and yet not lose her grip on the audience, she called above the music,

"Be seated, please." We all sat down immediately.

The procession, reassured, moved on slowly, and reached the front row, just as the pianist reached the end of Pomp and Circumstance. Evidently the presidents were coming up to take their places on the stage in the row of empty chairs on either side of me. The pianist tried a few chords to cover the ladies' deliberate ascent of steps to the stage, but the dignitaries had not the agility to meet this rapid impromptu. The leader paused disapprovingly and the line bunched uneasily behind her.

"Again," said the chairman, with a brisk wave to the pianist, and that uneasy moment passed. The pianist, after one or two irrelevant arpeggios with the right hand, while she turned back to page one, set off briskly on the second round of

Pomp and Circumstance. The leader of the presidents, startled but pleased, looked at the chairman. She evidently thought the instruction had been for her to lead her company around the hall again, and I think would have complied happily, but the chairman, deferentially though firmly, beckoned toward the platform. The leader gave in, mounted steps near the piano, and walked slowly across the stage to stand in front of the chair at the end of the row. When the last past president stood before the chair at the near end of the row, we all looked toward the pianist, who was well into the second page and giving herself completely to the music as she had not been able to do on the first rendering. Now she sat well back from the piano. Oblivious of the Women's City Club, she swayed to the majestic rhythm of the music. But the chairman's planned program did not include a second complete performance of Pomp and Circumstance.

"Thank you, Mrs. Kettery," she called, in full voice. She had to say it twice more before Mrs. Kettery came back to us and tapered off regretfully.

The chairman stepped from behind the lectern and stood beside it. Instantly everyone in the audience was either on her feet or attempting to be, including the past presidents on the stage, but not including me. I was somewhere away with Mrs. Kettery, and came back to the ladies only when I heard them say, in uneven unison, "I pledge allegiance to the flag."

I rose immediately, abashed because of my badly timed risings and sittings, and because I do not know the oath of allegiance to the flag. When I went to school it was not taught, and though I mean to learn it for occasions such as this, I forget my intention between occasions. Alone on the platform or with only a chairman near by, I mumble convincingly, but the past presidents to my distress were close in on either side of me. Their nearness made it difficult too for me to ascertain whether or not they were saying it with gestures. Some organizations do, and others do not, and I do not know whether it is more embarrassing to try to catch up with the gestures or be the only one making them. I have been in both positions. This group made gestures. When I caught up with them, each past president had placed her right hand on her left bosom. When they pointed to the flag, I was at the hand to bosom position, but we came out together at the end. We all sat down, though I waited until everyone else was seated to make sure that was what we were going to do.

The chairman took her place behind the lectern again, adjusted her bifocals and opened her black leather notebook. She made a pretty play of pretending to read from it that her present agenda said that today there would be no agenda, because this was an opening day party, and her agenda said that an opening day *had* no business agenda. We laughed so merrily over this sally that she had to rap her gavel to bring us to order again.

"But," she continued, "I have the very pleasant business and pleasure of introducing—" Before she could bring out my name, she was stopped by a disturbing sound from the wings on the left of us. She looked off uncertainly toward the sound. So did the past presidents and I.

"What's the matter now?" one of them said. They all craned forward except a tall, thin white haired woman on the end seat at the left. She rose to her feet, carrying a black hearing box in front of her and stepped authoritatively to look into the wings. On the way, she stopped to announce,

"It's Ella."

She disappeared off stage, but was back in a moment.

"It's Ella," she repeated. "She's got a message," and resumed her seat.

The chairman was trembling a little. She looked toward the wings and then down at the lectern. Perhaps she was hoping to find something in the rules of order book that would give her the support and technique for dealing with the unexpected. But her hat slid forward dangerously, because she had forgotten to move her head slowly, and the hand she put up to adjust it was trembling. She took a few steps toward the wings, and returned to the lectern. I think she lacked the strength to make the trip.

"Will you come out please, Ella, and deliver the message?" she asked, and her voice quavered.

Ella came slowly and shyly out from the wings. She was a colored maid, plump but trim in her starched white uniform. The importance of her message gave her courage, and though her eyes were wide with astonishment and dismay at finding herself out on the stage, she spoke up loud and fervently.

"Mrs. Woolston," she said, "should go right home. The doctor says it's mumps."

"If the lecturer is seen before the lecture it spoils the surprise—
people might turn in their tickets."

A girl with dark hair curling at shoulder length who looked not more than eighteen, stood up in the middle of a row half-way up the hall, and began edging past the knees of the members between her and the aisle.

"Tell Beulah I'm on my way," she called to Ella. "It's Billy," she explained. "I sent for the doctor before I left. I knew it was something."

"Yessum," Ella answered soberly from the stage, "I surely will," adding with charming dignity, "and ladies I beg your pardon for interrupting your proceedings."

As Ella left the stage, the lady with the hearing box stood up again and called to the retreating Mrs. Woolston, "Keep him warm, Caroline." Other members murmured their sympathy. Mrs. Woolston stopped in the doorway to thank them all and to apologize for having upset the meeting.

There was a chorus of assurances that indeed she had not and wishes for a light case. Mrs. Woolston left, the ladies settled down again and turned back to the chairman. The chairman's hat had got off to one side but she seemed unaware of it. She wiped her forehead several times and patted her temples with a small pale blue handkerchief.

"Ladies." She urged their attention again in a voice that quavered slightly. "I know we are all very sorry about the bad news which our dear member Caroline Woolston has just received, and we send her our sympathy, and Billy too."

The lady with the hearing box stood up. "I should like to propose, Madame Chairman, that the Club send the flowers to Mrs. Woolston that we always send to any member who is sick. After all, Caroline is going to be quarantined with that boy and he's a *limb*. She probably *will* be sick before she's through, and having to leave in the middle of our first meeting, I think we should send her our regular floral sympathy." Another member promptly seconded the motion.

A third lady protested vigorously that she thought it would be much nicer to send a toy to Billy and just sympathy to Caroline. A fourth member interrupted to say that that would establish a precedent and if they once began sending things to the children of the members just because they got mumps with all the contagious diseases there were for children to get, the treasury wouldn't have a cent left in it. Someone in the back of the hall proposed a series of bridges to start a "sick fund" for the children of members.

17

By now, the chairman was pounding a little hysterically with her gavel, and begged them all to come to order. Applying her tiny blue handkerchief to her forehead and temples again, she reminded them that this was not a business meeting and that they were all out of order. The result of this was an even greater protest, several members declaring acidly that the little Woolston boy's mumps could hardly wait for a business meeting. The chairman after an imploring glance at the book of parliamentary rules, declared that she would appoint a committee to decide whether Mrs. Woolston or Billy should receive an offering of sympathy from the club, and would ask the ladies to give a vote of confidence in the decision of the committee, empowering it to proceed. She appointed the lady with the hearing box as chairman. This suggestion was accepted and seemed satisfactory to everyone.

The chairman felt for her hat, gave up trying to locate it, and said,

"Ladies, with your permission, we shall resume the business of the afternoon, which, as I remarked, is not business at all, but our privilege and pleasure to introduce—"

The folding doors at the back of the hall

opened, a heavy set gray-haired stern woman stood in the doorway.

"Excuse me ladies," she said.

The chairman gave a slight scream. "What is it, Mrs. Hancock?" she said, and her voice was shrill.

"The other door to the lounge is stuck," the newcomer called from the back of the hall, "on account of that new painting job and the heat. There isn't any way we can get through to set up the extra tables in there, unless we go through here. It won't take us a minute. The girls have got everything ready and then when you're through your entertainment we'll bring the food in."

From my place behind the lectern, I could see the chairman's knees sag, but she put a hand fiercely on either side of the desk and straightened again.

"Very well, Mrs. Hancock," she said, and applied the blue handkerchief again. "I'm sure the ladies will understand the emergency."

All the ladies with a buzz of interest, watched the maids file through the hall, carrying table cloths, silver, trays of glasses, plates. They were followed by two porters, who made several trips with folding tables. Mrs. Hancock, at the end of some ten minutes, asked if there was anything more to come. A porter and one of the maids said they didn't believe so. Mrs. Hancock waved to the chairman.

"I hope we won't have to interrupt you again," she said.

She went out, closing the folding doors behind her.

The chairman took a deep breath, reached for her hat, failed to find it, placed a tiny ball of pale blue handkerchief on the lectern, and said,

"Ladies, on this happy occasion of our first meeting of the season, it is my privilege and pleasure to present——" and then she stopped.

"It is my privilege and pleasure to present," she repeated, and shook out the little blue ball, applying it to her forehead and temples. When she had finished, she waved the blue rag toward me in a wildly beckoning gesture.

"Honey," she said, half turning to me, "*you* tell them who you are, and what you do." With a last clutch at parliamentary form, she added,

"And it gives me great pleasure to present her with this opportunity of doing so."

A Railway Station, Every Time

A station does not have to be large to please me.

FOR THE PAST three years, I have been on a six to eight weeks lecture tour each winter, and I have enjoyed it.

My friends and family greet me on my return with a commiseration that embarrasses me, because it is wholly unwarranted. Traveling, they say, must be so hard—all those trains and the waits between.

Traveling on trains is my favorite activity, and I include in that, the waits between. I think very little, on the other hand, of a trip in an airplane. But that is because from the moment of boarding it, I take on a heavy responsibility. The pilot is not aware that I am sharing his burden, but I am not diverted for an instant from the things we have to do—get us off the ground, keep us in the air, follow the allotted course, maintaining a sharp lookout for weather changes and a keen ear for any off-beat in the roar of the motors, and bring us down, holding back against too swift a descent, to an accurate but gentle association with the narrow landing alley. Also, I have the conviction, which I do not expect science to justify, that if I hold my breath, I am lighter, and therefore easier for the plane to sustain.

With so many demands upon me, it is not surprising, I think, that a plane trip is tiring, but I ask nothing of myself on a train. From the moment I enter a railway station and hand my bags to the redcap, I yield up all sense of personal responsibility for any part of the trip, and step into a dreamy detachment from the world around me. This detachment has caused me, occasionally, to dream my way onto a wrong train or past the station where a lecture engagement and a reception committee waited. But the hysterical energy which these errors occasion is relatively infrequent. My prevailing status is one of somnolent and benevolent calm.

Not only does riding on trains exceed for me,

in all honesty, my enjoyment of the places visited, but railway stations are for me delightful places in which to spend the waits between trains, and almost any amount of time.

One winter my lecture schedule was such that I spent a considerable portion of the night, at least once, sometimes two and three times a week, in the Albany station. I do not know the City of Albany at all. I have, in fact, never set foot upon its streets, but I know vividly the New York Central depot there from trainsheds to newsstands, to benches to restaurant, and back. Not once, but a dozen times, I have sat on a stool at the counter in the restaurant, eating bacon and eggs, drinking a glass of beer and reading a pocket detective story purchased at the newsstand, and heard the train announcer call the stations to be visited by a train at the moment approaching Albany on its way to points west.

The first time I heard this particular train called I paid little attention until a familiar name sharply penetrated my ear, as a familiar name always penetrates, making me start with a quick catch of breath. Muncie, Indiana, was the name, which is the town where I was born. And I realized suddenly: That's 'The Knickerbocker' that comes into the Big Four Depot in the morning. That's the very train I used to meet when it brought my Father home from New York and a surprise for me from Schwarz's.

After that, I always listened at the counter for the announcement, and wondered how it would be if I moved on out to the platform, got on the train and arrived in Muncie the next morning instead of at the place where my lecture was scheduled. But I never did.

I know the station too, at St. Louis. That is much brighter and bigger than the one in Albany. It is in fact as big, as we might say in Indiana, "as all get-out" and it is very brightly lighted. The Albany station is dusky. The St. Louis one has, also, a great many newsstands and shops. So has the Columbus station. You come from the trains down an incline into the waiting room of the Cincinnati station and there is a picture theatre at the far side of it. Inside the theatre a large clock on the wall is brightly illuminated to remind you constantly that you are only waiting there for a specific appointment with a train.

A station, however, does not have to be large, with shops or motion picture theaters in it to please me. I like to wait in a small one. If it is so small as to be unequipped with newsstands, it is almost sure to be heated by a large coal stove in the middle of the room, and heated to such a degree that the outside of the stove is a blush pink, and the interior of the room around eighty-five. I am, of course, talking about stations in winter, since that is the time of the year I go lecturing. I would consider eighty-five degrees excessive in my own house, but in a railway station waiting room, I find it delicious.

Looking drowsily at the fat stove, I like to watch the brakeman come through the room and spit on the stove as he passes. We both enjoy hearing the spit sizzle and watching it bubble. I am roused from this happy apathy only by other travelers who quixotically prefer a cooler atmosphere. They walk briskly up and down the platform, pushing their heads up and their chests out. They seem to me to be not very bright, hanging on to that old cliché of fresh air being bracing and good for you. I do not wish nor need to be braced by air, and I am quite sure that its freshness, or lack of it, has had no effect whatsoever on my health, which is excellent.

Though pitying them, I could tolerate the sheep,

if they could get to their silly practices by any means other than the door, but each time one tramps out or in, he admits a rush of cold air that rouses me to a momentary wakefulness.

At one of these moments, I noticed a small, gray-haired woman at the far end of the bench on which I sat ruminating. It was in the station at Neosho, Missouri, and I had been deposited there at 10:25 on the night of January 22nd, to wait for The Frisco, the sleeper to St. Louis.

The taxi driver who had brought me from Joplin was congenial to a point of real compatability. In the first place, he had taken for granted that I would ride up in front with him, and immediately after settling me there, had asked if I had to have any fresh air. On my assurance that I did not, he had wound up the windows tight, turned on the heater full blast, and the radio. We had not felt it necessary to talk, and we enjoyed the trip. We told each other so when he packed my bags around me in the station.

There were two benches in the Neosho waiting room. When I came in, a tall man was stretched out full length on one of them, asleep. On the other bench a woman sat at one end, a man in the middle. I paid little attention to either of them as I settled in at the other end of the bench, put my feet up on one of my suitcases, tucked my hands into the sleeves of my coat and drew my head down into the coat collar. I looked at the stove. A dirty yellow cat lay almost against the fender and the stove was pink with heat. The cat lay on its back, its front paws curled, one dropping across the other, and it purred loud enough to sound like a neighbor's lawnmower on a shimmering, hot July afternoon in Indiana. Occasionally the stove popped, and I thought about Mrs. Draper.

Mrs. Draper would not have liked sitting in a hazy torpor in front of the stove there. She would have wanted to be doing something—but I liked Mrs. Draper. I had had dinner with her and Mr. Draper before my lecture. They had called for me at a quarter to six at the Hotel Connor.

I had met Mrs. Draper a few hours before that, however. She was the woman with gray hair who had sat in the back of the car when we drove from the station to the hotel and I had thought her shy. That had been at half past twelve, when I arrived from Kansas City and three members of the women's club met me. One was Mrs. R. K. McPherson. Her name had been

signed to my contract for the lecture. I reached
for the name of the second. She was young, slim,
dark-haired, and wore a cute hat,—but the purring of the cat, and the heat of the stove got in
the way of my remembering.

The third woman, however, was Mrs. Draper,
and as I climbed out of the car at the hotel, Mrs.
McPherson, who was driving, had said, "We
have a lady author too, in Joplin—Mrs. Draper,"
and nodded her head at the lady in the back seat.
Mrs. Draper nodded back in deprecatory gratitude at being identified, and Mrs. McPherson
returned with nods expressing, "Not at all,—we
are very proud of you, my dear."

When I said I was extremely sorry not to
know her books, Mrs. Draper spoke for the first
time. She would like me to come to dinner with
her and her husband, she said, and she would
bring a copy of her book. She'd only written one.
Mr. Draper would telephone me from the lobby
at a quarter to six, if that was agreeable to me.

Mr. Draper telephoned up to my room
promptly at a quarter to six. We would not eat
at the hotel, he told me when I joined him in the
lobby, because he and Mrs. Draper thought the
cafe was better. It had nice fish dinners.

Mrs. Draper was waiting for us in the car and began to talk, leaning out the car window, as we came through the revolving door. She had brought the book she said and handed it to me as I climbed into the back seat. She and Mr. Draper sat in front.

There were so many things she wanted to ask me, she said, that she hardly knew where to begin. Did I think the publishers were as smart as they might be about selling books? They were certainly nice, polite people, but she wasn't so sure about them as merchants. Her family had always kept store and she knew something about selling.

Did I take copies of my books with me—for instance, on the lecture tour? If I didn't she would like to offer it as a suggestion. She herself had been doing quite a bit of speaking recently and took a bag full of books with her wherever she went. But she never came home with a single one. She had no trouble selling them at all.

We had reached the cafe. Mr. Draper helped us both out of the car. When we got to the door, Mrs. Draper asked if he was sure he had turned off the ignition and the lights and did he have the keys? He showed them to her and she led the way into the cafe.

The cafe had a white-tiled floor, bright overhead lights and tables close together with a few booths. It was crowded at six o'clock, but we had a table reserved because Mrs. Draper said everybody ate at five thirty or six, and we wouldn't have had a chance of getting in otherwise.

Mr. Draper helped us off with our coats and hung them together with his own on a coat-rack. I had not seen him very clearly until then. He was tall, a little heavy, gray-haired and his skin looked as if he were outdoors a great deal. While Mrs. Draper decided what to eat, Mr. Draper told me that he wrote too. He was a newspaper editor and he did articles for magazines—trade magazines mostly, on subjects like fishing and outdoor sports, but he had never tried writing a book.

I looked at Mrs. Draper's. The title was "Though Long the Trail." She had given our order and was ready to talk about it. It was the story of her own mother's trip in a covered wagon out to California, and she had put it down just as her mother had told her. Then she had verified the places by going herself on the train, and every single place her mother mentioned was correct. The verifying was easy because the train followed a good part of the old Oregon Trail.

Mrs. Draper said that the first time she sent the book the publisher rejected it. So she went over to the university and took a course in writing under an excellent professor who told her that she was trying to be too literary. "I was too fancy," Mrs. Draper said. So she re-wrote the book three times, simplifying and cutting. "I took enough out to make another book and a half," and then the publisher accepted it. She smiled unexpectedly at Mr. Draper, and her eyes brimmed with tears. She explained, wiping them away with the palm of her hand.

"The night the galley proofs came Mr. Draper said he'd bring me down here to this very cafe and buy me a fish dinner. He did too, and we were so excited he left the lights burning on the car and the ignition turned on and then he locked the car up tight and left the keys inside. We never even knew it until we came out after dinner and then we had a dickens of a time. That's why I always ask him now if he's got the keys. But we were so excited that night we didn't know what we were doing. I don't think anything in the world can equal the pleasure of those long strips of paper with printed words on them that you wrote yourself. Do you?" That was exactly what I thought, I told her.

I asked her when she had begun lecturing and she told me she'd done that long before she ever wrote the book. That was when she had the idea that you could make clothes without patterns. She demonstrated it too. Sold the idea first to a department store and then to the Chautauqua. And whenever she went on the Chautauqua circuit she'd get a store in the town to furnish her material for the demonstration and lecture, so she had no expense in that regard.

But she'd found that the easiest way to talk, cutting and fitting at the same time, (she took a little niece along with her as a model) was to say something you knew by heart. So she'd written the whole speech in the form of a poem and could recite that without thinking of it.

She still liked to do sewing. She liked making all kinds of things, and she alternated that with the new book she was writing—so as to keep her hand in.

She and her husband had fitted up a room in the cellar, and they practically lived there during the worst of the heat in the summer. She liked to write lying down with a pad propped up on her knees, so she'd either be on the couch and her husband sitting up in one of the wicker chairs writing, or she'd be at the sewing machine, and he'd take the couch.

Just as I was thinking how much I would like to visit them one summer and do some writing myself, down in the cool room in the cellar where the wicker chairs were painted green and she had done all the upholstery, the pink stove popped again, and the man sitting in the middle of the bench jumped up and tramped over to the door. I knew then that he was one of the brisk ones. And sure enough, he pushed the door open all the way and started out on the taking-deep-breaths-pushing-out-the-chest program. The cold air whirled in around the room. The cat turned over, got up, stretched, and lay down again under the bench where the man was sleeping.

And the woman at the other end of the bench spoke. "I'd rather get home at two o'clock in the morning, than wait," she said. "I'd rather do it every time."

Now I was roused anyway, so I pulled my head up out of my coat collar and saw that she was small, plump, with white hair, and that she wore a very pale blue hat at a sprightly angle, and a gray squirrel coat. She had pulled the coat out from under her so as not to "sit out" the fur, and it spread up and around her like the back of an old-fashioned peacock chair. I asked if she had been waiting long.

"Five hours in this station," she said. This exceeded any sitting of mine, and she was aware of my respectful surprise. "I had such a time getting here," she explained, "that I didn't even want to risk going up town for a bite to eat for fear I'd miss my connections. And now it seems I could have taken a train that went through here an hour ago, only it would have got me home at two o'clock in the morning. The ticket agent didn't even tell me about it until it was too late. He said he didn't think I'd want to be getting in at that hour. But like I said to him, I'd rather get home at two in the morning, than wait—every time."

It was a soothing repetition, and the sound of it was difficult to untangle from the cat's purring. I slipped down into my coat collar again and half listened, while she told about busses, and seeing her brother in Yellow Springs in a house that had a gas heater in every room, which didn't seem

36

healthy to her and he didn't look any too well to her. The kids were kind of sickly too. And everybody in the town had told her a different way to take to get home until she was so mixed up that by the time she got to this station she didn't feel like moving any farther. Though if she'd known she could have caught the other train she certainly wouldn't be sitting here because she'd rather get home at two o'clock. . . .

I drifted out of hearing and when I came back she was talking about violas. This roused me a little because I would not have guessed her to be particularly interested in music and musical instruments. "I collect them," she was saying. "I must have forty or fifty of them right now in the bedroom." I thought she must be very fond of them to have them around her so intimately.

"Buster," she said, "that's my dog, he's part bull terrier, gets real jealous of my spending so much time puttering around my violas. I wouldn't let him in the room with them, he's so clumsy he might knock into them. He lies at the top of the stairway outside the door and pouts. I never saw such a dog for pouting. I'll bet he misses me too. I can just see him now, when I come in the door. He'll be laying up at the head of the stairs,

37

pouting, as sure as anything. I wish I'd got to go on that other train. I'd rather get in at two o'clock in the morning than wait,—every time."

The next time I listened, the words had to do with violas again and I asked her if she played them. She stopped talking so abruptly, that I looked over at her and she was staring at me sharply. "I tend to them," she said, "and they take a lot of care, the pink ones especially, and I've got my eye on some white, at least I've heard of a place where I think I can get them." Before I realized that she had been talking about flowers, a blurred but surprised picture presented itself of my friend, Mr. Samuel Lifschey, who plays first viola in the Philadelphia Orchestra, and his associates, exhibiting to the Friday afternoon audience, a motley of pink, blue and white violas. I explained quickly that I had misunderstood what she had said and she was reassured.

"They come in different sizes, too," she explained, and I started to tell her that Mr. Lifschey's was larger than the average instrument, but thought better of it and began to drift down into my collar again.

"I have so many customers," she was saying, "especially around Easter time. I expect there's

not many people in Muncie that haven't had one
of my violas some time or other."

I came up out of my collar and my torpor as
if the door had been flung open wide. "Muncie
where?" I asked.

"Why Indiana, of course," she told me, re-
moving, with her tone, the possibility of the ex-
istence of any other Muncie. "That's where I
live,—that's where I'm going now."

"That's where I was born," I said, "in Muncie, Indiana."

The man lying on the bench across the room
spoke. "A man come in here a few weeks ago
and stood over me. I was like I am now. First I
knew he was there I hear somebody say, 'Why,
hello, Charlie.' Sure enough it was a fellow I
went to school with down in Texas. You can't
ever tell, can you?" He went back to sleep again.

"What's your name?" the viola keeper de-
manded. I told her. "Well," she said, "I know
your family—every one of them. I guess you
must be Hal's daughter, aren't you? And don't
you do something or other?"

We went up and down Washington Street
and Main, and both sides of the block—square

we call it in Indiana—on Walnut Street, where she lived.

"You might have known my brother," she suggested. "It was his niece that I took with me. Left her down in Florida. She's a scrawny little thing. I took her in the berth with me going down to keep me warm, but I wouldn't have known I had anything in the bed. Didn't seem to give out any heat at all. I got sick, too. Train sick. I made up my mind it was because I was laying down."

The brakeman opened the door but I was awake anyway. "Train's coming," he said. The man on the bench sat up, stretched, and said he'd help with our bags. The cat came back to the stove again and curled up beside the fender.

We followed the man with our bags out to the platform and stood shivering while he made calculations about the location of our car. He guessed exactly right. The train pulled in and we were standing in front of the steps. The porter released the platform over the car steps, came down and placed the box for us to step on. The Pullman conductor followed him. I stepped aside for my friend from Muncie.

"I'm not going in the Pullman," she announced. "I've got a ticket, but I'm going to try the day coach. Is that the next car?"

The Pullman conductor was surprised, but said it was, and there was a little confusion while the door to the day coach was opened. The man from the station carried her suitcase over to the day coach steps, and swung it up to a brakeman. She climbed the steps nimbly and turned back to wave good-by to me.

"I'll tell people I saw you," she said, and I, climbing the steps to my car called that I hoped to see her some day, and her violas, and the dog pouting, in Muncie. The Pullman conductor was following me, and she leaned over and around her platform to send him an explanatory message. "I prefer to be sick sitting up," she said. And then she added, politely, "I *like* trains, though."

I like trains too, and railway stations. Every time.

"My Heart's in My Mouth"

I remember telling them to stand still, look up and speak out.

THREE YEARS AGO, an agent in New York communicated with me, and asked if I would like to go on tour under his management. I had never gone lecturing in my life except once when I went out on behalf of the school which my children attended, and spoke to alumnae groups, while we sat around at tea and reminisced over which of the old teachers were still there. Nevertheless writing on assignment for a good many years has induced me to accept practically any job, thanking the person deeply for having offered it. The consideration of my own ability to do the job has come quite a long time after. I once wrote an article on beagling, because an

editor asked me, and though I called the livery of
the beaglers their costume, and though I hope
never again to see a beagle, let alone, sobbing for
want of breath, follow one, it never occurred to
me not to write the piece when asked. For me,
then, to say to a lecture bureau that I knew nothing about lecturing would be very silly.

So I went to New York and told Mr. Leigh,
the head of the organization, that I would be
delighted to go on tour for him. What would
he like me to lecture on? That, he said, was entirely up to me. Would I submit to him a list of
subjects with provocative titles for them? I had
written a book with Cornelia Otis Skinner, and
another by myself. Therefore they would like me
to speak about anything I pleased. Lecturers evidently are not people who lecture. They are people who have done something else. That is their
qualification for professional public speaking. So
I signed a contract.

After all, I argued with myself all the way
home to Philadelphia, it was just like an editor
asking you for ideas for articles. You would give
the ideas and if they were approved you would
write the articles. This time, instead, you would
speak them. It was really just the same thing.

But I was not fooled, for one moment, by any such specious talk. There was all the difference in the world, the pit of my stomach told me, between a reader's turning past in a magazine, an article in which she was not interested, and an audience walking past, or out of, a lecture which did not appeal to it.

Nevertheless, the irrefutable fact remained that if I did do them I would be paid; and so as soon as I reached home I got to work. By the following morning I had a list of five subjects, really three,—three subjects about which I cared enormously and about which I had been wanting to write for some time: "Women Selecting Professional Jobs," "Women Doing Volunteer Work," and an article, or lecture, on careers which I had seen "a-borning," and the beautiful, though unconscious, pre-natal care which had preceded these births. Then, just as I always make up a big number to put at the top of any blank check which I write out in a shop, in order to give the impression that I write thousands of checks and have an enormous bank balance, I added two extra subjects, to make the number bigger. I thought, too, they would point up the worthwhileness of the other three, which carried a message.

So I put down "An Amateur Goes to Hollywood," and "Confessions of a Scapegoat." I then went into the matter of clothes, with equal solemnity.

Once, long ago, when I had had a job with Marshall Field and Company in Chicago, I had been asked to give a fashion show and talk on "Clothes for the Platform." I worked out a series of precepts which all came back to me now. "Do not wear," I had said sternly wagging a forceful and admonishing forefinger at an audience of women, whose youngest member was certainly twice my age, "any ornament which might distract attention from what you are saying, pins which catch the light and glitter, beads which can become tangled or break if fingered. The attention of an audience can be distracted by the slightest unusual movement, or light." (I had learned the facts from people in the theater. To be so pompous had been my own idea).

"Do not," was another of my warnings, "wear clothes which carry much detail. The audience will spend its time figuring out how the detail was applied and will come away with a lasting memory of it and a knowledge of how to copy it, but without the slightest inkling of what you were saying at the time." "And do not," I told them primly, "commit the gravest blunder of all. Do not wear clothes that are too short. Have your clothes for the platform made a little longer than those you would ordinarily wear on the street; because the height of the platform from the level of the audience makes a foreshortening."

Then I shocked them. "Use make-up," I said boldly, "whether you are accustomed to putting it on or not. You will have a stronger light on you than that in which you move about ordinarily, and your face will fade out. This is the time, on the contrary, when your face must be emphasized because your expression gives more point to what you are saying. Emphasize your eyes with eye shadow, eyebrow pencil, and eyelash make-up. Rouge is not so important as lipstick. Your mouth should be high-lighted in red like a Corot picture." That, I thought was a touch of culture that would bowl them over. "And," I harried them, "do not, if you wear a hat at all, select one with a brim; what features it does not entirely conceal, it will throw into an impenetrable shadow. Most important of all," I had concluded with a grand sweep, "whatever clothes you wear, *Leave alone*. Do not fuss with your shoulder straps, your belt, the chain of your lorgnette, pin, beads, or bracelet. Stand still, look up, and speak out."

There were other injunctions, of course. I had been asked to make my speech forty minutes long, but these were the highlights. And, remembering them, I thought they were still good. I bought clothes accordingly, two simple black daytime dresses, all line and very little trimming; one wool, one crepe and satin, and two black evening dresses, one black velvet, the other black crepe. The black velvet followed every precept; it was entirely without decoration, had a black net yoke, the velvet beginning with a fold just below the shoulders. The crepe, I was a little dubious about. It too was off the shoulders; but it had a red rose at the waist and another at the shoulder. I worried a little about the possible distraction of those red roses; but decided eventually to attempt to rise above, rather than sacrifice them. Since I wear, at all times, hats so far atop my head that I once in Hollywood took a shower with one on, I was not troubled by an elimination of brims which might hide my features. The features, such as they were, were accustomed to exposure. For make-up I went to my long-tried friend Cornelia Skinner. By this time I was carried away by my own advice, and assured Cornelia that I really thought that you could not use too much make-up. "Yes," she said, "you can," and vetoed artificial eyelashes. She agreed about everything else, however, from eye shadow to a brush in lieu of a lipstick, in order to make the line of the mouth smoother and more precisely where I wanted it, though, she said, it took practice to get it there. I bought the accoutrements, and I practiced. That completed my equipment. I was now ready, I felt, for the platform. All I still lacked were engagements.

These came so late, it was evident that I had been "taken," because no other speaker was available. The printed contracts, heavy with legal phraseology, carried in inserted typewriting, the date of the occasion, and the title selected from the list which I had provided, and certainly I need not have bothered about the ones with a message. The only titles selected were (a) "Confessions of a Scapegoat" or, (b) "An Amateur Goes to Hollywood." If anyone was interested in my earnestly considered opinion, he was not represented in these contracts. He was, however, and that pronoun I realize is sheer fantasy on my part, it was always a she who figured, interested in details which surprised me. I would not, she requested, speak less nor more than one hour. I would not read my speech nor, if I could help it, use notes. I would be prepared to use, if necessary, a microphone; or be able to speak without one. My social life was tabulated too. I would, so some contracts read, lunch with the ladies of the committee. According to others I would have a tea after the lecture, a reception if it were at night, or a dinner before the lecture. I might have instead, according to the contract, supper in my room at the hotel on a tray. "Of course," I said with pretty humor to Mr. Leigh, "I don't suppose they mean literally supper on a tray in my room in the hotel, I *could* go down to the dining room." "You could not," he told me firmly. "If they say they want you in your room, they want you in your room. You see," he looked a little apologetic but perhaps I only imagined it, "some of these organizations feel that if the lecturer is seen before the lecture, it spoils the surprise. People might even turn in their tickets." It seemed to me a drastic reaction to one look.

Obviously I did not, after that, even inquire as to a possible leeway permitted in the choice of clothes. The typewritten memoranda read, "Afternoon clothes," "Street or day clothes," "Formal," and there I was ready for them. Formal would be, for me, the black velvet; or all out with the red roses. Day clothes, very simple, but "molded" creations in wool, satin and crepe. Afternoon clothes troubled me. I had not thought of these as something apart. In my normal life I would be apt to wear in town, in the afternoon, approximately the same thing I would wear if I were going in in the morning; but, for this division in time, I scurried out and bought another dress. It had a pink bow, but I overrode the principle of no decoration, with the assertion to myself that it made the dress look further along toward evening. My preparations were made, my designations were in my hand, and I started out.

The fact that I forgot to take along my contract to the first engagement is, I think, irrelevant. I was, it is true, rendered unaware of the name of the place where the lecture was to be held, the name of the organization holding it, and of the hostess running the affair. This lapse, however, only forced me to canvass timidly the hotel lobby, which I did remember was the place designated for my meeting with the committee for the luncheon, and inquire of each female citizen established there if she were looking for a lecturer. I was fifteen minutes early, the committee ten minutes late. By the time we had established contact I had compiled enough answers to make up a Gallup poll, all of it negative. This, however, I maintain, had nothing to do with my sensation when the moment came and I was standing on the platform about to lecture. I was in day clothes without ornament. My hat was without a brim. My eyelash make-up was so heavy I could barely see my way to the lectern. But the trouble did not stem from my equipment, it came from my hands and my heart. My hands were eerily cold and disagreeably moist, and I found it troublesome to swallow, because my heart seemed to be in my mouth. At that moment I, who would rather be given an opportunity to talk than play any game known to man, would have preferred a hundred times to be on a galloping horse with a polo mallet in my hand, than be on that platform about to speak. I, who would not for *all* the king's horses, care to straddle anything more enterprising than a burro. But the high romantic ideal, which has sustained me through so many crises, came once more to my aid. "You're being paid to do this job," the still small voice informed me. "Go ahead and do it."

And so I began to speak,—haltingly and then, I think, with greater sureness, until I forgot about having to swallow, and was interested in my audience instead. I wanted those people to be interested. I wanted desperately for them to be amused. The only excuse in the world that I had for being there at all was to divert them for a little while from the gravity and tenseness that surround in these days, our waking hours. There was a ripple of laughter. Never again let anyone tell me about peaks on which they have stood, Alpine or Darien. I was on them all. By the time the lecture was three quarters through, I was so far above myself that I decided to try something else, something I wanted particularly to tell, because it had made a very deep impression on me. It was not funny, but I would try it.

I would like, I said, to recapture a little, if I could, for them the opening day of the shooting of the picture "Our Hearts Were Young and Gay." I had not, I explained, known what scene was to be taken first, because, as I was sure they all realized, the scenes were not done in sequence.

All of those which took place on a particular set were "shot," followed by all those which took place in another background. I had heard that the opening day of shooting, however, was a little like a first night in the theater. The executives came over to wish everybody good luck, flowers were sent to the players, and there was a general air of tension and excitement. I anticipated this as I stumbled along through the enormous, dark warehouse which Hollywood, in a unique moment of understatement, calls simply a stage. Finally I made out a circle of lights at the far end, and when I came, at last, into its radius I did find the executives and the flowers there. But I found also that the scene was to take place in the cabin of the ship in which the two girls were sailing for Europe. And I found that the cabin duplicated, to the tiniest detail, the very one in which Cornelia and I had set out. It was perfect in every detail, down to the water bottle tilted in the little wooden container, the narrow, white upper and lower bunks; obviously we were traveling in the most modest circumstances.

In the center of the room the girl who plays the part of Emily, was waiting for the word to begin the picture. She was dressed in a costume,

By the time I was three-quarters through I was far above myself.

which to the last stitch, was a replica of the one which I myself had worn. Just as I stepped within hearing the director said, "Ready, camera. *Roll em.*" And Emily spoke the first words of the picture as it was shot. They were the words which I myself standing in that very cabin, dressed in that very suit had said to Cornelia, twenty years ago, "Cornelia, I can't believe it's true. Emily Kimbrough's going to Europe."

For one blinding, electric moment I was the young girl standing there. Nothing that had happened to me since that time, was real at all. Europe lay ahead with all the excitement, beauty, and adventure that being young could bring to it. It was all to come, and I was on its threshold. That was a shaking moment, and I tried to capture something of its quality, for this audience, telling it falteringly and stumblingly, as one does, I think, the things which lie very close.

Suddenly I was aware that what I had once been told about, was happening to me. A response was coming up from someone in the audience, a response so vivid and actual that it was as if someone had put a hand on my arm and said, "I know how you felt. I had a trip of that sort when I was young; and if I should see it recaptured I think it would be almost too sharp to bear." I looked about to find, if I could, from what particular person this could have come, meantime going on with my story. I found her, even through my mascara, sitting on the end of the first row, watching me with an intentness which made me know at once that the curious communication had come from her. I was sure that she was living again in her own mind, some such voyage, and was moved by the memory, because I even thought I saw, by the reflection against the footlights, the shimmer of tears in her eyes. Then she closed her eyes and leaned her head against the wall. And her head pressed the button which set off the fire and burglar alarms.

There was no instruction in my contract, to cover this tattoo. So I stood there while the braying, jarring clamor swelled. It must, I thought, stop at some time and I would be ready, when it did, to go on as if nothing had happened. This, I had understood, was the law of troupers and I would prove myself one. It did stop and I started; but it turned out to be an intermittent alarm which died down only long enough for me to hurl two or three words into the quivering silence, before it caught up with me and passed me easily. I suppose it actually must have stopped eventually. I only know that when the firemen, the police force, and the insurance representative came pouring into the back of the hall, I left the stage with a curious bow, which I suppose I intended to imply as a gesture of farewell to the audience and welcome to the civic authorities.

I have never since then been so confident in a lecture, nor so nervous before one. It gave me the conviction into which no human being could have exhorted me, that nothing so appalling could possibly happen to me on the platform again. I tremble, as I write this, and pause to knock on wood. I did feel that *other* things might, and probably would, happen, but nothing on so wide a scale. And that is a very calming thought. And that is the way too, it has been, so far. Other things *have* happened, but not of such grandeur. They have been of a more personal nature, resulting principally from that lecture wardrobe which I had assembled by such splendid precepts.

The first of these lesser occasions was at an afternoon lecture when I wore the black wool street dress, so devoid of distracting ornaments that even the buttons were down the back. One of these buttons capriciously and without precedent twined itself into my hair, which I wear in a somewhat Victorian knot low on my neck. I could have borne the discomfort more placidly, had my head been in a normal position, but in some quixotic fashion, the button gathered to itself individual, and evidently very young, tendrils when my head was lowered, so that to raise it severed these tendrils one by one and excruciatingly. Therefore lest I break into a yell of sudden pain, I was forced to finish out the lecture with my head pushed down as if I were suspended from the hook of a coat hanger. And I could encounter my audience's eye only by looking cautiously up, from under my eyebrows, with unexpected and idiotic archness.

It never occurred to me to give a trial lecture in my bedroom wearing the black velvet evening dress. I had tried it on, but I daresay I stood still in the fitting room. I do not, as a matter of fact, whirl about on the lecture platform, but I did reach forward, the first night I wore it publicly, for a glass of water, placed conveniently on the lectern. I could not, however, pick it up, because I was not able to lift my arms. The velvet band which ran around the base of the net yoke below the shoulders, was as inflexible as those iron bands which Mr. Longfellow's blacksmith possessed. I could put my hand on the glass, but I could not lift it. And that fascinated the audience. Everything I had once said about the distraction which clothes can cause was being proven, with conviction and humiliation. I was also wearing a pair of combs trimmed with brilliants. I thought that much ornament in the back would not be distracting. It was distracting, however, to have one of them fall to the floor, and in all the years I have worn them, that had *never* happened before. The audience divided itself into titters and cooing noises of sympathy over my effort to pick it up, and my inability to reach the back of my head with it. I should, of course, have left it on the floor. But I was so surprised that I stooped spontaneously, and certainly I held the audience spellbound. Never, of course, have I had so many other inclinations to raise my arms. My nose suddenly began to itch intolerably, and I cannot remember ever before having that affliction. One little hair was, or felt as if it were, brushing across my forehead, and another explored the rim of my ear very delicately. But I stood pinned down, and immobilized, except for a spasmodic and involuntary twitching.

Nothing untoward happened the first day I wore the black satin and crepe afternoon dress. This was the model which depended entirely upon line. I was depending a good deal upon the dress too, and at the end of the lecture was rather pleased the way we had both come out.

It was then that a woman from the audience came up to shake hands and said, "How different you look off the platform, Miss Kimbrough. I wonder if it could have been the dress? Up there, you know, you looked the way people do in front of those broadening mirrors at amusement parks."

Now that is the aspect of lecturing to which I am not as yet accustomed. It did, of course, require the services of the police and fire departments to reconcile me to the unexpected incident. But either I have not as yet encountered that peak in the observations made by members of the audience, or else any or all of their unexpected remarks are not the equivalent of the fire and police department.

"You have something to live up to," the president of the club said, as we sat at lunch. "Our *last* program was *such* a success." "Really?" I asked nervously. "What was it?" She sighed happily. "Chief Eagle Plume," she answered, "in an evening of War Cries and Dances."

"Tell Miss Skinner," a woman called out across the crowd at an after lecture tea, "that if I had gone on the stage, as I had wanted to, I might have been her mother. I often think of it." She sent a little twittering wave of her hand to me, and left. I find myself thinking about it often too; but I have not as yet told Cornelia.

I did tell her, however, and Roland Young, because we were talking about remarks which could not be answered, about the woman who said I was such a nice person. "I said to myself," she had asserted, pressing my hand with real affection, "all the time I was listening to you, 'Now that is not what *I* call funny but she seems such a *nice* person, and I am just going to tell her so.' " That, Cornelia said, was one of the unanswerables, and there were many of them encountered by all public performers. Not so long ago, she remembered, a woman had approached her at the conclusion of the performance, and taking one of Cornelia's hands, placed it upon her very ample bosom or somewhere between, had patted it, saying over and over, "My dear, my dear, my dear."

Cornelia challenges me to find a response to that, and *I* cannot. Furthermore Cornelia insists the gesture itself was not easy to answer. How long should she have left her hand there for patting, or should she have perhaps brought the other one up, of her own volition, to keep it company?

I remembered, too, the inspired introduction which the chairman of the evening gave to one of Cornelia's first performances. "Ladies and gentlemen," she began, and stopped. It was evident that she had forgotten her prepared introduction. She started at the audience, drew a deep breath, and said what must have come from the subconscious, and the heart. "Due to the exorbitant price of Admiral Byrd, we have with us this evening, Miss Cornelia Otis Skinner."

Roland Young tells of a man who came up to him in a hotel lobby and placing his hand upon Mr. Young's shoulder, looking him up and down from head to foot, ejaculated with obviously the greatest pleasure and friendliness, "Yes *sir*, yes *sir*." Mr. Young is a careful and deliberate man, and he is still deliberating over the courteous reply to that expression of recognition. It has not, however, as yet occurred to him.

65

They are just like the imponderables which I face with unallayed trepidation, but with anticipation too. I was standing by the hostess, after my speech, meeting the guests as they came in. One of these, a pleasant looking woman, spoke to the hostess and shook hands with her conventionally. Then she turned toward me. "This is Miss Kimbrough," the hostess told her, and the guest shook my hand with equal conventionality. But instead of speaking she unexpectedly closed her left eye in the most debonair wink, tossed her head and made an extraordinary clucking noise three times, as if she were urging on a horse. Perhaps I should have winked and clucked back at her. I did not, however, make any response whatever except to continue shaking her hand in a rather hypnotic, mesmerized fashion. And I do not know what I should have done, or said.

I am far from complaining about this form of social communication. I have the deepest gratitude to anyone who comes up to speak at all, and a feeling of sympathy for them which I can scarcely restrain myself from expressing. I have been a member of an audience so much longer than I have addressed one, that my feelings are entirely below the platform. There are few things more distasteful to me than going to the speaker, or the actor, after his performance. I have not the slightest idea in the world what to say. If I tell him that I liked it it sounds to me lukewarm, as if I really had not cared for it at all. But if I say I adored it or "loved every minute of it," I seem to be gushing like a girl, which I am not, and therefore am once more confounded by my own awkwardness. Deepest of all I have a conviction that the performer is scarcely going to alter his work according to whether I liked it or not; that his indifference, in fact, to whatever I may say or happen to think about it is cosmic in proportion. Brooding over these conjured up reactions I am therefore, by the time I have reached the object of my back stage pilgrimage, in such a state of sullen gloom that it must be only too apparent to the performer, if he should happen to notice, how desperately I wish I were anywhere but facing him. No wonder then that as a performer my heart, that unstable organ, goes out in sympathy but in gratitude too, to any member of my audience who should have overcome his reluctance and marched along to say anything at all. Certainly his heart is in the right place.

Luggage for the South

"Got your empties?"

On January 26th, 1945 I was in Shreveport to give what my agent with conscious humor calls a lecture. I had been giving a great many of these lectures, that is I had been giving this same one a great many times, though not always under the same title. I was, in fact, on a lecture tour, my first. I carried my itinerary in a leather case, especially made for it and given to me for Christmas by my daughter, Margaret. The outside flap of the case was stamped Emily Kimbrough, but on the inside the stamping read Mrs. Kimbrough Wrench, Haverford, Pennsylvania. Evidently Margaret's feeling had been that a professional name was all right on the surface, but for genuine, practical identification, no such nonsense. The itinerary was compiled and bound in blue paper by the lecture bureau, but I had drawn it out so many times to check on my passage from town to town that the edges were curled up and the color very dirty. My repeated withdrawals of the itinerary were perhaps exaggerated by the circumstance of my having forgotten one lecture. I had forgotten it actually, because that daughter, Margaret, had developed an acute attack of appendicitis and been operated on at four o'clock in the morning of the day I was to appear at the Newark Women's Club. The lecture bureau was very kind about my omission once they found the reason because, they said, it was a reason made to order for women's clubs. Nevertheless it was not a reason that I felt I would be able to use often and the incident made me jumpy about my engagements.

To get to my Shreveport appointment, I came down from Flint, Michigan on a Wednesday night arriving at the Dearborn Street Station in Chicago at seven o'clock the following morning. I had pulled out my itinerary so many times that I knew even the place on the page where it said that I would leave Chicago from the Union Station at 8:15 A.M. That gave me one hour and a quarter in which to change stations, with very little leeway if the train were late. The train was not late, but I was the first one off, scuttling up the steps beside the porter, and urging him on with sharp cries as if I were driving a dog team. The result was that I reached the Union Station with time to spare, and so I telephoned back to my house in Philadelphia to give messages, and to hear once more the voices of my dear ones before I dropped down into the far off south. We clung to each other over the telephone until I had only five minutes left, and then I wrenched myself away, hurried through the gate into the parlor car on the first lap of the trip, which was, so the itinerary said, Chicago to St. Louis.

A man was sitting where my ticket read I should be. The conductor, summoned, was apologetic. The man and I were both gracious about it. It was the kind of thing, we said, that happened frequently nowadays. It had, however, I interpolated gently, never before happened to me. I was on a rather extended trip, I told them, my accommodations had been reserved by an organization, and never before had there been an occasion of this sort. The man bowed himself away, saying that in that case the mistake obviously was in his ticket. I settled in, relinquished my slip to the conductor, and hoped to him politely, that the other gentleman would be able to find a seat.

In St. Louis I had a wait of three hours. I took a long walk, and sent back to the twins some candy from a shop I came upon, which the St. Louis girls at boarding school used to talk about.

When I got on my sleeping car for Shreveport, I found my berth occupied. The conductor said he was very sorry but that it did happen occasionally in such busy times. Meantime the man in the lower berth was struggling back into his clothes behind a curtain that bulged and writhed like the Laocoon, or like a man putting on his trousers in a lower berth. The conductor talked to him from our side of the curtain, explaining that my tickets had all been purchased through an agency for a long tour, therefore the chances were that my accommodations were correct and his single purchase was the one in error. The man agreed docilely and with apologies for having usurped my place. He went off down the aisle, carrying a shirt, collar and tie over one arm, his coat over the other shoulder, his hat uncertainly on his head as if he had tossed it there as a place to hold it and as if it had barely caught on. He carried a small valise and walked down the car with his neck thrust out to anticipate the hat's falling off. The porter followed with a large bag.

When the berth was made up again, I settled into it and had a comfortable night. But the porter told me next morning that he never had been able to find another place for the man, not even an upper. He had had to sit up the rest of the night in the men's room. I said that it was such a pity that inexperienced clerks these days caused such things to occur.

The train came into Shreveport at half past eleven, three hours late—that was very good, the porter and the taxi driver said. The day was warm and sunny. I could see from the taxi that the streets were wide, but that there seemed not to be very many of them, nor any trees along them except one row in front of the Court House. In the Washington-Youree Hotel, a large crowd of people was waiting to register. I made no effort to find a place. The lecture bureau always secured my reservations well in advance and I had never had any difficulty. When my turn came I simply

75

said to the clerk, "You have a reservation. My name is Emily Kimbrough."

He smiled back at me, "Yes, Miss Kimbrough, indeed we have." I felt a pleasant glow of contentment at being so taken care of. The clerk poked his fingers in and out of little pigeon holes, drawing out scraps of paper, reading them and putting them back. He paused over one and came back to where I was standing.

"Miss Kimbrough," he said, "we have a reservation for you for Monday."

"That's quite right," I told him, "I'm here."

"Miss Kimbrough," the clerk said, "this is Friday."

All the other people waiting to register stopped talking among themselves and looked at us. So did the cashier and the telephone girl and the clerk who handed out room keys. There was nothing I could think of to say to the room clerk that would make any sense. If you have amnesia, I wanted to tell him, there would be days behind you which were obliterated in your mind. What kind of disease could you have when there were three days ahead of you for which you could not account? It was, of course, nonsense to speak of the fourth dimension, but I couldn't help thinking about it. I said aloud,

"My schedule says that I arrive in the morning and lecture that night at eight o'clock. 'Evening dress requested. Organization will call for you at the hotel and escort you to the club.' " The itinerary was always rich in detail.

The clerk repeated, "That's right, Miss Kimbrough, Monday. Today's Friday. But," he added with the pleased surprise of a child, "we can give you a room just the same, where you can wait until Monday."

I wondered if he thought it would be better for everyone if I were locked up in it until then, but I only told him faintly that that would be very nice.

When I had got the bellboy out of the room after an interminable fussing over how to open the window and showing me where the coat closet and bathroom were, side by side in a total area of five feet, I sat down in a rocking chair by the window. I sat there for a long time without doing anything at all, because I couldn't think what to do. First of all I couldn't think how I could possibly be here on a Friday when it was meant to be Monday. Then I couldn't figure out what the lecture bureau had done with those three days. I still had on my hat and coat; I'd thrown my bag on the bed. I got up from the rocking chair by the window, went over to the bed, pulled out the leather container once more, extricated the dog-eared and dirty itinerary, followed with my finger down the page to Flint, Michigan—to Chicago. I had read it over a hundred times, except for the left hand column, which had seemed repetitious. I read that now in order not to leave a word unturned. It read: (left hand column) "Thursday, January 25th (night of 24th), (middle column) leave Flint, Michigan, Grand Trunk #5, (right hand column) 12:45 a.m. (left hand column) Thursday, January 25th, (middle) arrive Chicago, Illinois, Dearborn Station, (r.h. column) 7 a.m." And then my finger shook. The *left* hand column read, "*Sunday,* January 28th, (middle col.) leave Chicago, Union Station, Alton Railroad #19, (r.h. column) 8:15 a.m., (middle) arrive St. Louis, Union Station, (r.h. col.) 1:45. (l.h. col.) Sunday, January 29th, (middle col.) leave St. Louis, (r.h. col.) 5:50 p.m. (l.h. col.) *Monday,* January 30, (middle col.) arrive Shreveport, Louisiana, (r.h. col.) 8:30 a.m."

78

Left hand column: Thursday, January 25, arrive Chicago. *Sunday,* January 28, *leave* Chicago.

Three days in Chicago. Three beautiful days in Chicago where I used to live, where my parents live now, and beautiful friends. Three days of idleness arranged with thoughtfulness by the lecture bureau to take place in the one spot where I would like to be, with time to see everyone and not a single job to do. Shreveport was lovely, so I had heard. But I couldn't very well tell the woman in charge of the lecture that I was three days ahead of time. No chairman could be expected to cope with that disaster. Three days alone in Shreveport. Of *course* my seat was occupied in the parlor car to St. Louis; of course another man had my berth on the train from St. Louis to Shreveport. Why hadn't the conductor looked at the date on my ticket? Why hadn't I looked at it for that matter? But after all that was part of a conductor's training. I certainly needed training, too, in reading. Why hadn't my children at home when I talked to them on the telephone in Chicago known that I shouldn't have been in such a hurry? They had a copy of the itinerary. I found later that they *had* me paged in the Union Station in Chicago, and had then given up. The dolts. They know now about sending a telegram to a train. The name and number of the train were right there before them on the itinerary. I could have been snatched back at St. Louis and restored to Chicago. But I was not in St. Louis. I was in Shreveport, Louisiana. After I had sat a long while in the rocker by the window, thinking about these things, I thought about lunch.

The dining room was large and very decorated. I ordered salad and a bottle of beer.

"We don't serve beer in this dining room," the head waiter told me.

Beer happens to be the only thing I drink, but I do like that and if ever there was a time when I wanted it, it was then. I got up from the table.

"Never mind the lunch," I told the head waiter, "I'll try the other dining room."

The other dining room was the Coffee Shop. I sat up at the counter, and ordered salad and a bottle of beer.

"We don't serve beer here," the waitress told me, "only in the bar."

"Never mind the lunch, thank you," I told her and got up from the stool at the counter.

The bar was alongside the Coffee Shop. Over the doorway, a neon sign read "Ladies not permitted in the bar without an escort." I went back to the Coffee Shop, and told the waitress about the sign.

"That's right," she said, "you have to have an escort." I asked if I could get one of those but she didn't answer. Then I asked if there were any way that I could get beer out of the bar to me. She came back at that and suggested that I go to my room and try Room Service. I left the counter once more, went out into the lobby and up to my room. I ordered from Room Service a salad and a bottle of beer. Room Service said the hotel only carried draught beer which couldn't be taken out of the bar. I said,

"Never mind the salad," and hung up.

Walking down the street I wondered if I were putting too much into getting a bottle of beer, but it had after all given me a purpose with from Friday to Monday to carry it out.

The first few places I tried had no beer. I think it was in about the fourth place that the proprietor said that they did carry it, and gave me a choice of brands. I ordered twelve bottles, in my relief and pleasure. The proprietor put them up on the counter, cold and wet.

"Got your empties?" he asked genially.

I began to feel a little of the fourth dimensional again. I told him that I did not have any empty bottles if that was what he meant. He began putting the beer away again. He was sorry, he told me, but he was not allowed to sell beer unless he had the empty bottles in return. It was all I could do to keep from leaning on my stomach across the counter and snatching them back again. It was suddenly, too, all I could do to keep from crying. I told the proprietor that I had traveled all the way from Philadelphia and that I had not carried empty bottles as part of my luggage.

"That's too bad," he said, "because we can't sell 'em here without we get the empties."

The last bottle was gone from the counter, back down into the ice below. I went out of the store and up the street. It was very hot. I had on the only coat I had brought, my best one, and that was mink.

Two or three blocks farther on I found a place that sold beer, but they wouldn't sell it there without the empties. It was at the fourth place after that one, that the proprietor agreed to sell me a dozen empties. He couldn't sell me the beer too, he said, but he would sell me the empties and I could take them back somewhere else and exchange them for beer. He brought out twelve empty beer bottles and at that moment I felt I had never seen a prettier sight. I paid for them and then he said,

"Where is your carrier?"

"My what?" I asked him.

"Your carrier," he told me impatiently. "Something to put these in. I can't sell beer bottles to you unless you have something to take 'em away in. It's not allowed."

I was afraid I might cry again.

I explained that I had traveled from Philadelphia and had not brought with me a carrier. He was sorry, he said, but that's the way it was. He couldn't sell beer unless the customer provided a carrier, basket, like. I asked if he knew of a place to buy a basket. He couldn't think of any at the minute. I asked him tartly, I was so hot and tired, if he could give me the address of a weaver and I'd get one made. He ignored that. As I started out the door, he softened. I could try the market down the street, he called after me.

"Might be they'd sell you a container. Ginger ale carton or anything would do."

I nodded, because I couldn't speak, and went on down the street. By this time the heat was so intense that it made the street and sidewalk look ridged as if they'd just had a permanent wave, and not a good one. Sweat trickled down the back of my legs and itched. When I got into the market I found it so crowded that I had to wait a long time before I could be served. I asked if I could have a ginger ale carton and the boy shook his head. I was defeated by now beyond argument. I turned and started away. He called after me,

"Not without you buy something to go in it."

I caught sight of a box of cheese crackers on the shelf, dropped it into the ginger ale carton at my feet, and asked if that would do,

He said, "Sure," and charged me ten cents for the cheese crackers, twenty-five for the carton. I went back along the sun-ridged pavement, my hair wet and sticking to the back of my neck. The proprietor, who had said he would sell me the empties, was behind the counter, just as I had left him, his head leaning on his open hand, his elbow on the counter. He did not change his

84

position, but he brought out from under the counter with his free hand, twelve bottles, one by one. He packed them in with the cheese crackers, and I went out on the street again. For the first time I began to have misgivings about the number I had ordered. Twelve empty bottles seemed heavy.

I went on a quarter of a mile farther to the last place that had offered me cold beer, if I could supply the empties. The man remembered me and pulled out the bottles as he saw me come in the door. He was fat with white skin, little blue eyes puckered in at the top of sagging pouches, and strands of black hair arranged like Venetian blinds over the glare of his shining bald head. I handed over the empties and he replaced them, bottle for bottle. I was so hot that the sweat was running down into my eyes. I had to wipe across them and my forehead before I could actually see to count the change. I put my bag over my arm to make room for the carton, and inched the carton off the counter onto my own front, sagging under the weight. The sweat ran down my legs. A strand of wet hair tickled my nose. I couldn't let go the carton to push it back.

The proprietor came round from behind the

counter, and delicately lifted the strand into place. Then he was suddenly at the door, the knob in his hand. Until that moment he had been almost without motion, but he swept open the door, and bowed with a flourish like someone out of Margaret Webster's "Shakespeare."

"Good day to you, Madam," he said, "I hope you will enjoy to the fullest extent the cheer of the beer, and the hospitality of our southland."

My chin was hooked over the edge of the carton to help balance it, so that I could only mumble, thank you. I was also too surprised to think of anything else to say.

Out on the street, the carton kept my coat pushed back on either side, but the sweat trickled down everywhere and itched, especially under my girdle. My hat was uncomfortable, too. When the man replaced my truant strand of hair he had jogged my hat a little so that it had slipped back. It felt the way the hat had looked on the man leaving the lower berth in the train, and I had to stretch my neck the way he had stretched his, to keep the millinery balanced at all.

The hotel was eight blocks away. I felt with my foot for each curb, because I couldn't see over the carton, and I counted them. When I came into the lobby the mail clerk called out,

"Have a nice walk? You look hot. How do you like our Southern climate?"

I relaxed the grip of my chin on the carton enough to smile, but I didn't say anything. It wasn't much of a smile either.

Up in my room, I eased the carton onto the wash basin. I was afraid if I bent over to put it on the floor, I couldn't get up again. I sat in the rocking chair by the window until my legs had almost stopped shaking, and then I went over to the telephone by the bed and called Room Service.

"I would like to order lunch," I said, "just a bowl of green salad."

"I'm certainly sorry," the operator told me, "but the dining room is closed."

After awhile I ate the box of cheese crackers, sitting in the rocking chair, and drank quite a lot of the beer.

"Cincinnati and I"

The janitor and I salvaged my belongings from the rubble.

Not long ago, I returned from a six-weeks lecture tour, and, looking back on it, I feel that two facts emerge emphatically: first, that I am what my Grandmother Kimbrough used to call "not right sharp" about schedules, and second, that Cincinnati and I are not happy together.

On this tour, I had my second lecture date in Cincinnati. My first was in 1946, when I arrived there on February 26th at 8:30 a.m. from an engagement in Pittsburgh the night before. That time, I stayed at the Netherland Plaza. This season, I was at the Hotel Gibson. I can understand, in view of my demolition of a portion of the Netherland Plaza, why the lecture bureau should have put me in another hotel on my second trip. But until the morning of October 31, 1947, I thought that the grotesque 1946 Cincinnati incidents were only a kind of three-day northeaster that had blown itself out there. In the light of what happened this year, I am inclined to believe that Cincinnati is a storm center for me and that hereafter I will do better to skirt around it.

The 1946 grotesqueries actually began on February 25th, on the day train from Philadelphia to Pittsburgh. I was well along in a six-weeks tour. It had been strenuous but, on the whole, pleasant and uneventful. I had had a week-end interim at home in Philadelphia, and was starting out on the middle lap of the tour, rested, and comfortably settled in my parlor-car seat. I was, I remember, knitting when I first smelled smoke.

Craning my neck around toward the back of my chair, I sniffed. I could not smell any smoke there, and none of the passengers were sniffing, so I went back to my knitting. Then I smelled it again, and this time I was sure that it came from burning leather. I summoned the porter and said to him that I didn't wish to alarm either him or the other passengers, but did he smell smoke? He chuckled reassuringly, but stopped abruptly to point to a thin line of smoke that was drifting up from the mouth of my black suede handbag, which I had wedged between my chair and the window. It was a bag I kept out of sight as much as possible—a difficult thing to do, considering its size.

The bag had been made in Hollywood at a famous suede shop, and it wasn't finished until the day I left for the East and the lecture tour. I had ordered a pouch-style bag, with suede draw-strings long enough for me to wear over my shoulder. It was to be eight inches wide and ten inches deep, but when I went to the shop to get it—one of the fifteen last-minute errands that day —I found the saleslady holding it in her hand and looking at it in awe. At the sight of me, she said, "Miss Kimbrough, I don't know if you'll want this. We've got a new cutter, and I think she's exaggerated." We measured the bag, and it was twenty-two inches wide and twenty-seven inches deep. I took it, because there was no time to have it changed, but I kept it out of sight whenever I could.

The porter grabbed the bag and turned it upside down in the aisle. Besides the ordinary things any woman has in her bag—purse, compact, lipstick, cigarettes, Kleenex, handkerchief, theater-ticket stubs, shopping lists, and swatches of material—there was a large tin of Postum and a folding spoon. I do not like to admit that I cannot drink coffee, and the suede pouch had seemed a good place to hide the Postum I always carry with me. This time it didn't work. The tin rolled all the way down the aisle to the men's room.

The last thing to come out of the bag was a book of blazing matches that had burned through a corner of the lining and into the suede. It took a great deal longer to gather up the items shaken out in the aisle than it did to stamp out the fire, although the other passengers pitched in and helped. After I had thanked them all and explained about the Postum and the size of the bag, I was glad we were coming into Pittsburgh.

The clerk at the desk of my hotel sniffed a little while I was asking about my reservation, so I felt that I had to explain the episode to him. The bellboy, too, wanted to know about the smell, so I held the bag up for both of them to see. Once in my room, I bathed, dressed (formal evening dress requested, it said on my contract; women's clubs are always explicit), had my dinner sent up, and was called for at half past seven by the chairman of the evening and her husband. He was, he told me, in charge of the backstage arrangements, and he proved to be very genial. I constantly marvel at the patience and cooperation of the husbands of women's club ladies. This Pittsburgh husband delivered me and his wife at the door of the auditorium and joined us backstage after he had parked the car. He asked me how I wanted the lights, and since I know nothing whatever about lighting, I said that I thought overhead and footlights would be just right, and he said that those were exactly what he had turned on, which I had noticed. His wife interrupted us with the announcement "If we wait for latecomers, the early ones get restless," and strode onto the stage. I followed her.

We got off to a fine start. Her introduction was hearty, and she remembered it. "It gives me great pleasure—" she ended, and we bowed each other into reverse positions, she to the chair I had quitted and I behind the lectern.

About three-quarters of the way through my lecture, I had occasion to illustrate a point I was making by holding up my hands on either side of my face, like blinders, and in doing this I leaned my elbows on the lectern. There was a ripping, crunching sound, and the lectern disintegrated under me. The rim, breaking up into pieces that looked like the kind of kindling wood that is full of nails, flew down into the front row, where the unhappy people dodged in surprise. For a moment, it looked as if I would join them there. As the lectern sank to the floor, its component parts spreading out at my feet, I lost my balance and gave every appearance of an inexperienced diver about to plunge reluctantly over the footlights. But by rotating my arms vigorously —though I was hampered by the tightness across the upper arms of my off-the-shoulder dress—I brought myself back to an upright position. I had, however, lost the thread of my lecture, and so had the audience. I made a few efforts to find it but it seemed better just to wish them good evening and leave the stage. Their sportsmanship brought me back to take a bow. The janitor accompanied me, and after my bow we both squatted down while he helped me paw out from the rubble my handkerchief, gloves and bag— not my knapsack but a small evening bag that was harder to find. He helped me to my feet and glared at the audience.

"I told you ladies to tell your speakers not to touch that lectern," he shouted. "It's got worms in it."

The chairman and her husband were garrulously distressed all the way back to the hotel. He said she ought to have warned me, but she said that because she'd noticed I didn't carry notes, she'd thought I probably wouldn't lay a hand on the thing, and hadn't wanted to make me nervous.

I boarded a late train that night, slept fitfully, and rose early to get out at Cincinnati at seven-thirty. Following the redcap who had my bag, I stepped briskly along the corridor that leads from the train sheds into the main waiting room. The floor of this corridor is smooth white marble —or something like marble—and felt slippery. It dips down decidedly the last few yards before you get to the waiting room, and when I reached this incline, I veered to the left impulsively to walk on a black band about two feet wide that extends the whole length of the corridor. I thought it was a rubber carpeting put down as a safeguard against slipping, but it was of the same kind of stone—apparently just a decorative note. I had hardly set a tentative foot on it when something caught me behind the knees, upended me, and carried me on it smoothly down the slope and into the waiting room, my feet in the air and my hat over my face. I heard running footsteps behind me and a man's voice calling indistinguishable words.

As I was slowing down to a stop a hand grabbed my arm and pulled me to my feet. I pushed up my hat and looked into the anxious face of a Marine. He was out of breath, but he apologized and explained in a rush of words that his bag here—he pointed to the piece of luggage on which I had just been recumbent—was so heavy that when he saw the incline ahead he had set it down, hauled off, and given it a big boot. Then I had crossed over without warning in front of it. . . . And if there was anything he could do. . . . He hoped I knew how bad he felt to have done such a thing. . . .

I think he was going to offer to see me to my hotel, but as I was assuring him that I was not hurt, a lady's troubled voice interrupted us. "This *is* Miss Kimbrough, isn't it?" She injected a nervous giggle. "I was just *sure* it was." After she had introduced me to two friends on the hospitality committee who had come with her to meet me, I turned back to the Marine, but he had gone.

We four ladies rode together to the Netherland Plaza in a car belonging to one of them, who drove. I was put into the back seat with the lady who had claimed me, but the driver and her friend in the front seat were so interested to know how I had "*ever* happened to come down into the station on top of that big black bag" that they kept turning around, in order not to miss any of the story. I am always nervous in a car I'm not driving myself, even behind the most skillful of drivers, which this one was not, so I was tired when we reached the hotel. The ladies said that they would come back for me about half past twelve to take me out to their club for the luncheon before my speech. The driver interrupted with a suggestion that if they came a little early, she could point out the sights as we drove along, and perhaps take in one or two places not directly on the route. In the face of their enthusiasm, I could hardly say that if I were given my choice, I would prefer to start out right then on foot, however far the club might be. I promised to be ready when they came, and they drove off, waving.

The luncheon was no more shrill than any women's gathering. The hostesses were charming and hospitable. My speech passed off uneventfully, and we had tea afterward. My ladies would have taken me out to dinner, rounding up some of the other "girls" to go along, but I told them about my Great-Aunt Wilmina, who lives near Cincinnati and was coming in to have dinner with me at the hotel, so they drove me back to the Netherland Plaza. When I left them, I said emphatically that I wouldn't dream of allowing them to go to the inconvenience of driving me to the train; I was leaving early in the morning for Louisville, and it would be much simpler for everyone if I got a taxi. They were prettily reluctant, but I was firm, and we parted with a rondo of good-bys and thank-yous.

Aunt Wilmina came to dinner, and I saw her off in a taxi at nine-thirty. When I got back to my room, I was tired, and very thirsty after a day of talking. I felt that I could drink an entire quart of ginger ale, and perhaps two, so I telephoned for two quarts, and a waiter brought

*have the deepest gratitude to a member of my audience who comes
up to speak at all.*

them. I asked if he had an opener, and he told me there was one in the bathroom.

After he left, I found the opener in the bathroom—a metal lip an inch and a half long, fastened with two screws to the frame of the medicine cabinet. One of the screws was loose and the opener sagged, but, nevertheless, I slipped the cap of the ginger-ale bottle underneath it and pulled down. Nothing happened, so I took a firmer grip on the bottle, inserted it again, and gave a quick jerk with all my strength. The opener came away from the medicine cabinet and fell into the washbasin. So did the quart of ginger ale, and with such force that it split the washbasin into two parts. One part toppled over into the toilet and splintered. The other dropped against the side of the bathtub and broke into four large chunks. The ginger-ale bottle was not even nicked, but the cap was loosened enough to send the liquid in a thin, powerful stream toward the ceiling and all over my head. It shot up with such violence that I couldn't pound the cap on again. I covered the top of the bottle with my hand, but the liquid squirted out over my dress, legs and feet. Ginger-ale is sweet and sticky, and there is more of it in a quart than I had ever dreamed.

When the last of it was out of the bottle, I mopped up as much of myself and the floor as I could with the one towel the ginger ale hadn't reached. Then I went into the bedroom, called the desk, and asked the clerk if he could spare the time to come up for a moment, because something had happened that I found difficult to explain over the telephone. When he arrived, another man was with him, but the clerk did not say who he was. I took them to the door of the bathroom and pointed to the empty ginger-ale bottle, which I had set down on the shelf above the toilet, thinking that if I started with the bottle, I could perhaps describe the accident step by step, and thus make it sound credible. The strange man picked up the bottle and held it all the time I talked. He kept looking at it, and then at the walls, where the ginger ale was dripping, and at the floor, where the remains of the washbasin lay. When I had finished my story, the clerk said that nothing like this had ever happened in the Netherland Plaza before. This did not surprise me. He also said there wasn't another room available in the hotel and that they couldn't get the washstand replaced that night, which also did not surprise me. He would send up a chambermaid to sweep up, he said, and to give me fresh towels. The other man was still holding the ginger ale bottle when they left. He hadn't spoken at all.

The chambermaid wanted to know what in the name of conniption had happened, and when I explained it to her, she said that it didn't seem to her it could have happened that way. But she telephoned the linen room to send me a box in which to pack the clothes I was wearing, because, she said, I certainly couldn't wear them again before they had been cleaned and couldn't pack them with my other clothes; the best thing would be to mail them home. She got the bathroom pretty well mopped and swept, and she brought me fresh towels. But she cautioned me not to step on the floor in bare feet, because there might still be a lot of chips around.

As soon as she had left, I got out of my clothes and into the tub and washed my hair. It took three separate washings and rinsings to get all the ginger ale out. My hair is long, and it was three in the morning when I had finished drying it. I put in a call to be waked at seven o'clock, because I was afraid I might oversleep and miss my train for Louisville. I caught the Louisville train by running up the incline at the station and all the rest of the length of the marble corridor.

When I reached home, a couple of weeks later, I found a letter from the Netherland Plaza Hotel. It read:

> Dear Miss Kimbrough:
>   On February 26, while you were a guest at the Netherland Plaza in Room 2522, it appears that you broke a lavatory in the bathroom. The cost of replacing this lavatory is $55.17. We trust that we will receive an early reply.
>   Yours very truly.

I replied, protesting the charge, because, I explained, the accident had been caused by a defective opener that was the property of the hotel. "I do not therefore feel responsible," I wrote, "though I regret exceedingly that it happened."

A week later, I received a courteous answer cancelling the charges for the broken lavatory. One more letter from me, thanking them for their understanding and generosity, presumably closed the incident. This year, though, as I said, I was booked at the Gibson Hotel, and I do not know whether it was by request of the Netherland Plaza or because of a delicate sense of consideration on the part of the man in the lecture bureau who makes my reservations.

I think I shall remember for a long time that I arrived in Cincinnati for my lecture there this season on Thursday, October 30th, at 6:20 p.m. I spent that evening at the theater, where I met some old friends who were in Cincinnati for a brief visit. They were at the Netherland Plaza and were sorry I wasn't staying there. I said only that I was comfortable at the Gibson and had stayed at the Netherland Plaza on a previous trip. They insisted on taking me back to their rooms after the play, and I looked wistfully around the familiar lobby as I went in.

I did not leave them until long after midnight, and found, when I got outside, that it had started to rain. My taxi-driver said he would just as soon it rained hard for the next twenty-four hours, on account of its being Hallowe'en the next night. He explained that the whole downtown district of Cincinnati was always turned over to Hallowe'en celebrations. Everybody came out, either in costume or just to see the sights, and the crowds were so heavy that taxis weren't even allowed on some of the streets. He said it seemed like anywhere you wanted to go, it took you ten blocks out of your way to get there, and, what with the crowds, you couldn't get through anyhow. But that was the way Hallowe'en was in Cincinnati.

I was very sleepy the next morning. I had breakfast in my room, got into a gray wool dress that, with gold necklace and earrings, was as near as I could approximate what was stipulated in the contract as "short, formal, daytime dress." I glanced at my lecture-bureau schedule hastily to make sure of the hour and address. It read, "Friday, November 1, Cincinnati, Ohio, Southwest Ohio Teachers' Association, 9:30 a.m., Scottish Rite Auditorium." By rushing, I managed to get to the Scottish Rite building at nine-twenty. It is a very large place, and I had some difficulty in finding the way to my auditorium, which was a lesser one. I had particular difficulty because there seemed to be no one else going there. I came upon it eventually, through a door that took me onto the stage, and found myself alone, except for a janitor who was sweeping one of the aisles. I asked him what was going on, and he said nothing, as far as he knew. He was irritated, because his back had been turned to me when I called him, and he said I had made him jump. I had no trouble finding my way out of the building, but it was hard to get a taxi. It was still raining and there were puddles on the sidewalk. I was wearing thin, black suede, open-toed slippers, and the water splashed in the toes and up over my insteps. As soon as I got back to my hotel room, I telephoned Mr. R. W. Cadwallader, whose name, as Executive Secretary of the Southwestern Ohio Teachers' Association, was on my contract. Mrs. Cadwallader answered the telephone. She didn't know where Mr. Cadwallader was, she said. Had I tried the auditorium? I told her I had. Well, then, she said, she didn't know where to find him, he was so busy with these meetings. Up to this moment, I had been calm, I think, but now I became a little high-pitched. Could she tell me, then, I demanded, where I was supposed to be? My lecture engagement was at nine-thirty and it was now quarter to ten.

"Wait a minute," she said, and left the telephone. In a moment, she was back. "I'm looking at my bulletin," she told me, "and you are speaking at the Scottish Rite Auditorium tomorrow morning at nine-thirty—Saturday, November 1st. I'm reading it right here."

"I'm sure my schedule says Friday, November 1st," I said, and I think my voice was trembling.

Mrs. Cadwallader was patient. "But Friday isn't November 1st. Today is Hallowe'en—you know, the thirty-first of October. Tomorrow is November 1st."

I was sitting on the edge of my bed, and after I had put down the telephone, I kept on sitting there for some time. I felt suddenly overdressed in formal daytime dress at 9:50 a.m. in a hotel bedroom, and I had twenty-four hours to go. Of course this was the thirty-first of October! The taxi-driver's talk about Hallowe'en the night before should have warned me. But it was Friday. I looked at my schedule again. It read, "Friday, November 1." I took out my pencil and corrected the schedule to read, "Saturday, November 1." It was too late to do any good. I should have checked and corrected my dates long before, especially since, on a previous tour for the same lecture bureau, I had got to Shreveport, Louisiana, three days ahead of time. But that mixup was my own fault. This at least was one-half the fault of the lecture bureau. I studied the schedule again and tried to figure out why I had been rushed from Mansfield, Ohio, the day before if I was to have a twenty-four-hour wait in Cincinnati. I had had to leave Mansfield in the middle of lunch after a morning lecture and drive fifteen miles to catch a New York Central train at two-ten, in order to reach Cincinnati at six-twenty on Thursday, October 30th. They knew I had a great-aunt near Cincinnati. I had written about her. They thought I would like to see her. As simple as that! It suddenly occurred to me to wonder whether my Pullman ticket for the train that was to take me to my next engagement might not be wrong, too. I got it out of the leather folder in which I always keep my tickets, with the schedule and my lecture contracts. It was for New York Central train No. 405, leaving Cincinnati for Chicago at 3:20 p.m., Saturday, November 1st. They knew, then, all along, at the lecture bureau, that I was speaking on November 1st, and that it came on a Saturday. Friday was just a slip of the typewriter—or a Hallowe'en prank.

I know now that it is not enough to read my schedule carefully; it is necessary to check it with the railroad accommodations. I evidently learn one thing at a time. It has taken two visits to Cincinnati to show me that that city and I do not blend.

LOVE — on a Train

"Get me back on that train!"

INASMUCH AS TRAVELING by train is my favorite activity, I am surprised by my own incompetence at it. I have always been of the bland opinion that if you like very much to do a particular thing, the chances are that you will do it pretty well. My dealings with trains tend to shake that opinion.

My chances of boarding and leaving the proper train at the proper time have dwindled until the margin for error has crowded the actual schedule almost off the page. Paradoxically, too, the more I travel, the more easily I am addled by a schedule. Time was—and there were railroad trains then—when I went East from Chicago to boarding school, later, over the same route, to college, later still, over the same route to Chicago from the East, with my children, to visit their grandparents, and never knew confusion.

I did lose one of my twins once in the drawing room, when I went into the lavatory to warm a bottle, but my only confusion in that instance was because I could not believe that in such a small space, a nine months old baby could be lost, and kept counting the same baby twice, until I held her under one arm, made sure there was no other visible, and discovered the truant happily asleep in a far corner under the berth.

Prior to that, in the boarding school and college era, the journeys home were so lacking in confusion, so established in precision, that they included ceremonial observances. We got off the train at Harrisburg, ran at top speed the length of the platform and up a long steep flight of stairs ——this was, indeed, a number of years ago——and bought a bag of fresh, hot, thick pretzels of a dour, thin man at the top of the stairs, who dispensed them from a basket. We came back to our car at the same speed, and I never heard of anyone's missing the train. We then ordered ginger ale, and settled down to enjoy the exquisite combination of ginger ale and pretzels, an enjoyment enhanced by the fact, we admitted, that we were the happy few sophisticates who knew about the man at the head of the stairs. It took me twenty years to experience that same complacent pleasure again by learning to order, on The Chief, immediately after leaving Chicago, Colorado mountain brook trout, to be served on the day it (presumably) is delivered to the train en route.

Somewhere in the years between those two achievements of sophistication, I remembered one day about the pretzels, just as the Pennsylvania train on which I was traveling from Philadelphia to Chicago, pulled into the Harrisburg Station. I leapt out of the train, went quietly up the steps, and found the same thin, dour man with his basket of hot pretzels. As he handed me a bag of them, and my change, he sighed unhappily. "Aren't you through yet?" he asked.

I look back on that unhappy incident with, however, a modicum of comfort, because it assures me that I was at least still on my toes about a schedule, if not about a flight of steps. That is no longer true. I am conspicuously down at the heels when traveling.

I start out on a lecture tour with a crisp, fresh, typewritten schedule, and the certain knowledge that for six weeks I will be on a train for some part of nearly every twenty-four hours, and the uneasy suspicion that at several parts of that six weeks, I shall be on the wrong train.

I hold, unfairly, the lecture bureau partially responsible for my degeneration, because its transportation department favors single spacing. The schedule takes up less bulk than double spacing would fill, but to read it requires the aid of a ruler, or a piece of string, held down by my thumb at the name of the town, and pointed toward the date and hour of departure which are listed at the far side of the page. I do not ask for larger type. Among many of my contemporaries, I have achieved a spirited unpopularity by the fact, which I take particular pains not to conceal, that I do not as yet require glasses for reading. But I find it difficult to follow straight lines in almost any department, and on a schedule, I am habitually diverted to the line above or below.

I can communicate this waywardness to others, too. In Alabama a short time ago, I took care of a baby on the train while his mother took a nap. I let her sleep until the train was pulling into the station. I put on the baby's bonnet and coat, and gathered up the paraphernalia without disturbing her—she had had no sleep the night before, she had told me when she handed over the baby. I roused her at the last minute. We were in the day coach so we had no porter, but other passengers helped us with our luggage. I hustled her, dazed and stumbling, out of the train. We were momentarily stopped, and she was further confused by a group of ladies at the foot of the car steps, with a photographer come to meet me and make a souvenir of the meeting by a group photograph showing them clustered about the steps with welcoming hands outstretched as I descended.

A baby in my arms was a surprise to them, and one which they did not wish to include. But after the baby was whisked out of sight into his bemused mother's arms, the photography and greeting were quickly done with. I retrieved the baby and went ahead with the group, the baby on my arm, the mother some distance behind us. The ladies went back for her and brought her to the taxi where I was waiting with the baby. I asked where she wanted to go, and she told me she had to wait two hours for a bus, and would like to see about getting her baggage transferred, but she did not know where she could warm the baby's bottle and feed him. I suggested that I take the baby on to the hotel, give him a bath and his bottle there, and she come on later— she could learn the number of my room from the clerk at the desk, and I gave her my name.

The ladies thought this all very sensible, the mother was pleased, and the baby and I went off to a very Morris Dance of waving handkerchiefs and hands.

Fortunately, the baby had had his bath, and very nearly finished his bottle, when the mother came back on the gallop to tell me that I had got her off the train two stations before the one at which it had been her plan to disembark.

It is perhaps just as well that ordinarily I hold very little communication with the other passengers. I am, I think, at most times gregariously inclined, but on a train, I am overtaken by a shyness which makes it difficult for me to decide what topic to broach, and during that period of indecision, the traveler across from me at the table, or next me in the club car, gets up and walks away. I have no difficulty in deciding what to say if anyone speaks to me, because no one ever does. I see other people speak to other people, but not to me. Except the man on the train from New Orleans to Jacksonville.

He was in the club car, and so was I—across the aisle from him, but I was on the wrong train, due to the single spacing on my schedule. It was a Sunday night, the eleventh of January. I had come into New Orleans the morning before, on the tenth, at seven-fifteen, and gone to the Hotel Roosevelt, as the schedule directed. This was the first time I had been in New Orleans, and I had longed for years to visit it. I stopped at the newsstand on my way to breakfast to buy a copy of every guide book on sale there. At the table I read bits from each of them, and twice I took out my schedule from my bag to see how long I was to stay, so that I could portion out my time for sightseeing—Sunday, January eleventh —Leave New Orleans, (L. & N. Station) L. & N. RR #38-3, 10:30 P.M. And this was Saturday morning.

By ten-thirty I was in the French Quarter. I would have been there earlier, but I had thought it would be picturesque to ride in an open trolley, and the trolley turned away from the French

Quarter at a demoniac speed. I lost considerable time getting back to my starting point.

From then on the day was perfect. I explored a considerable part of the Quarter on foot, stopping unashamed in the streets to read from the guide book, until, at the very moment when I was tottering from fatigue, an open carriage drew up alongside. The driver, knowing somehow that I was a tourist, volunteered to drive me. He was charming and very well informed. His name is Andrew Bailey and I wrote down his address, 2040 Panger Street. I lolled in the carriage as we drove, pushed the guide books to the floor, and tried to think of myself as La Flamme.

I succeeded to the extent of turning away from a little tea shop, when I had quitted the carriage at two o'clock, and lunching instead at Armand's on clear soup, fish with a sauce aumondine, green salad, and a little white wine, and crême brûlée. Had it not been for the carriage ride, I would have eaten a toasted cheese sandwich in a place with booths and a soda fountain.

I dined that night, and very well too, at the Roosevelt, and strolled up the street afterwards to see the picture, "I Know Where I'm Going."

Not only that, I had an ice cream soda afterwards
—chocolate.

It was all wild, careless fun, because I was in
New Orleans, and because for the only time on
this lecture tour I was in a city for two whole
days—with no professional engagement. My
schedule had firmly before this dazzling inter-
lude, led me to a sleeper directly from the lecture,
or to packing and early bed for a before-the-din-
ing-room-opens departure in the morning. But
on Sunday morning I woke to the lovely prospect
of another day, still in New Orleans, and I had it.

At ten fifteen Sunday night I was in line at
the L. & N. Station, submitting my railroad and
pullman tickets to the two judges who sit on a
platform in railroad stations at night, recite to each
other the numbers on the tickets presented, and
hand down a decision to allow the passenger to
proceed—or not. At 10:16 a decision was
handed down against me. The judges held my
pullman ticket between them and showed me
how it was stamped L. & N. RR. #38-3, 10:30,
January 10th. At 10:30 on January 10th I had
been viewing with an untroubled, happy heart,
"I Know Where I'm Going," because my schedule is typed with single spacing, and because I

find it difficult to follow a straight and narrow line.

The judges requested me to step aside, but to stand by their box for further pronouncement. I stood by, and watched all the other passengers present their tickets, and pass. Once, when I was ten years old, I thought I was not going to get from 4-B to 4-A, and the feeling was exactly the same, but at 10:25, the judges, after long deliberation, passed me, with a condition. If the party for the lower berth ticket dangled before me, did not turn up, I could have it—not 'til after the pullman conductor had made a complete check up, though, and I would wait in the club car! I think that part of the condition too, was that I should make the train in such a way as to give them some enjoyment in return for their trouble.

At any rate one of them said, "you'll have to run," and they both set off ahead of me. I ran, hopping over the tracks between the judges' bench, and my train on the farthest track. My overnight case whacked against the back of my knees, my fur coat slipped through my arm and trailed on the ground except for the corner which I ground into my side with my elbow. The lock on my typewriter case sprang open as I jumped a track, but I held it together by hitching the case up under my other arm—and I caught the train, with the porter scooping me up his steps to the car platform, where I stood wheezing while he gathered up my bedraggled equipment.

I was still wheezing when the man in the club car spoke, which made it difficult for me to hear what he said—but it was something like, "Nice going." I said, between gasps, "Why thank you. It was a close call. I was supposed to be on another train."

"That's how I had it figured." He nodded his head two or three times in a very apparent approval that pleased me, though I tried to be deprecatory and modest. I was pleased, too, at being spoken to at all, so when he asked if I would care to have a drink I told him I believed I would have a glass of ginger ale. Not to accept food or drink from a stranger is a law of traveling I learned from my parents in the days when we all knew someone who knew friends of the family of the girl who was drugged into the White Slave traffic that way. I have handed down the law with firmness and awful threats to my own children, but the possibility of my achieving such a fate now,

is remote. Nevertheless, I said to myself that
I would watch his hands every minute, just in
case. That is why I noticed almost immediately
that the tip of each finger on one hand had a letter tattooed on it. It took me a little time, even
with the unwavering scrutiny I gave it, to put
together the letters into the word L O V E. But
I considered it such a disarming exposure of sentiment that I relaxed at once. The man himself
was not very clean, but neither am I after a long
trip, which was what he was making, I decided,
though I did not ask.

As a matter of fact, we had very little conversation. I was overtaken by the old shyness of not
knowing what subject to broach that would interest him, and he seemed to catch the affliction
from me. Several times he started to say something, and stopped. When the pullman conductor arrived with the news of a berth for me, the
L O V E man was evidently pleased, because he
nodded quickly several times and leaned across
the aisle to whisper to me, the L O V E fingers
cupped around his mouth. "Never asked a thing,
did he?" I wondered if he were a European, un-
used to American traveling without passports and
permits and endless checking, but although I am

cursed with an irresistible desire to be helpful, I felt shy about giving a travel talk.

When I had failed to find anything to talk about, I thanked him for my ginger ale, and said good night and left for my berth. He said nothing at all, not even good night.

I slept late the next morning, went in to the diner for a sustaining double duty brunch, because we were due at Tallahassee at one forty-five and I did not want to eat again before or immediately after my arrival. My host of the night before was at the far end of the dining car, but did not answer my good morning, so I decided not to breakfast with him, but I saw that he was watching me as I ate, and I was, of course, pleased.

We were a little late getting into Tallahassee and I heard the conductor say to the porter who was unloading me from his car, that they would have to wait now for some other train to go through, and there was an awful lot of stuff to pick up, so they'd be held up plenty.

Tallahassee was warmer than New Orleans had been. Actually, it was hot and sunny. I looked up and down the platform because a note on my contract had said that members of the Books and Authors Committee would meet me.

That would have been the day before, of course, and perhaps they had made plans for my sched- uled Sunday stop-over here. I thought it would be pleasant to sit in the sun for a while on a bench and tactful, too, in case they tried again.

It was pleasant. I watched the men unloading baggage from the train I had just left, and other men waiting with truckloads to be put on. When this grew a little boring, I thought of the memo- randa from the lecture bureau which had accumu- lated during the trip. This would be a good time to sort them out and clip them together, throwing out the ones already taken care of. I am not usually so methodical, but with time on my hands while I waited for the ladies' possible arrival, I became very efficient.

At almost every hotel at which I stop on the tour, there is mail waiting from the lecture bureau. This invariably consists of a memo- randum to the effect that my lecture will take place in the High School and not the Presbyterian Church as originally planned, or that the club has decided to choose another topic in place of the one first selected. Since someone is always kind enough to act as host or hostess and deliver me to the appointed place, it is of no importance to me whether that place is the High School or the Church, and since the chairman may decide just before she and I step out on the platform that she would like to announce a topic on my list other than the one first selected, I do not regard the lecture bureau memoranda as irrevocably important, and so I pay very little attention to them.

But sitting comfortably on the bench, with a hot sun against my shoulders, I read them attentively and I came upon one which read, "The Tallahassee lecture has been cancelled. Will you therefore remain on the train from New Orleans, not getting off until Jacksonville."

I was off the train, however, on a bench, with my luggage piled around me. I looked up at the train, my train, on which I was to remain until it reached Jacksonville—and it was easing out at that instant, on its way.

I leapt to my feet, the memoranda fluttering around me. I yelled—and the conductor heard me—"Get me back on that train. I can't stay here."

The porter heard me, too. Nearly everyone heard me, and someone of them signalled the engineer. He stopped the train so vigorously that it squealed back on its haunches. The conductor and the porter ran to my bench, grabbed up my bags and ran back to the train. I gathered up the odds and ends—even the memoranda, and pounded after them. There was no time to put the stool down again, so they dropped the bags, boosted me up, heaved the bags after me, and swung themselves on as the train picked up speed.

The berth I had occupied from New Orleans to Tallahassee was taken from Tallahassee to Jacksonville. The conductor suggested that I wait in the club car until he could find another space for me. We were both out of breath, and he sat down beside me in the club car to rest a minute. He wanted to know what in the world had made me change my mind so suddenly, if I would excuse his asking. I said I did not mind in the least, but when I started to explain about the lecture tour, and expecting to be met because the contract had said I would be, and the single spaced schedule sheet, and the memoranda, it all seemed so complicated that I was not sure I could make it clear, especially when I was out of breath. I said, therefore, that Jacksonville had seemed, suddenly, to be a pleasanter place than Tallahassee in which to be. Just an impulse—everybody had one sometimes, didn't he think? He guessed that everybody was entitled to, certainly, and went away to find a pullman space for me.

That was when I saw that there was one other passenger in the club car, sitting in the chair next to the one the conductor was leaving. The passenger was the L O V E man, and the letters were twinkling when he put down his newspaper and picked up a glass. A hand moving about with L O V E spelled on the fingers gives off a kind of air wave of outgoing sympathetic understanding to which I was drawn, and I smiled at the man. I could explain everything to him, though I had not been able to unravel it for the conductor.

"I wasn't supposed to be at that station," I began.

He picked up his newspaper again and L O V E sparkled toward me. "You can get to be too smart," he said.

The observation confused me, and for that reason, put up a barrier between L O V E and me. I could not think of an understanding answer, nor did it show me the way to fresh topics. Consequently, I sank under the old wave of shyness.

After a few minutes I tip-toed out of the club

car, hoping he either would not notice my going, or would coax me back with an easy opening.

If he did notice me tip-toeing past him, he gave no sign of it. I sat in the ladies' room until the porter tapped on the door to tell me that the conductor had a berth for me.

I did not see the L O V E man again. I thought about him, however, all the time I was waiting in the ladies' room, and, intermittently, during the rest of the tour, because I was sure that he had been interested in me in New Orleans and put off by something in Tallahassee. It could not have been the lack of efficiency and the all-over incompetence in my character only too apparent at Tallahassee, because he had said I could be "too smart." I would not have said that I had given any evidence of it.

Three months later, a story in the Los Angeles Times corroborated my first impression, and, however unwarranted, bestowed on me a not inconsiderable measure of self-esteem.

PORTLAND, Ore. A Missouri kidnap suspect is in jail here today.

The FBI said the suspect is John Harvey Bugg, 31, object of a two and one-half year nation-wide hunt as "The man with love on

130

his fingers." His left fingers were tattooed with the word "L-O-V-E."

FBI Agent Howard I. Bobbitt said Bugg is accused of disarming Dade County (Mo.) Sheriff Hugh P. Wilkerson as the Sheriff was taking him to jail on a forgery charge Nov. 29, 1945. He forced the Sheriff to drive to Oklahoma, robbed him and left him tied to a Kellyville (Okla.) utility pole, Bobbitt said.

Mr. Bugg did want to ask me something in New Orleans, something very particular. I think he was considering me as a partner, perhaps a helpmate, because he admired the way I got out of New Orleans. But when he saw the way I left Tallahassee he decided I was too risky. When he said, "You can get to be too smart," he made up his mind to go it alone.

To think that someone considered me, even once, too risky, and that I might get to be too smart, gives me a feeling of considerable exhilaration. And I think about it frequently.

A Hotel Is Never Like Home

In no time at all they can give any hotel room a look of home.

When I step off the train, and for six weeks in the fall and again in the spring, I step off a train at least once nearly every twenty-four hours, I am met by someone from the organization sponsoring my lecture. If the membership of the organization is made up of women, I am met by a group, if men are "having me," a man, usually without assistance, takes over the job of welcoming me. A man is a particularly pleasant sight to see when I stand abashed in the center of a ring of luggage, all mine. Porters are scarce and women make fluttering and scattered motions of carrying the largest bag between two of them, calling nearby cab drivers to help, and waving me off when I grasp even the overnight case.

None of this is done in silent motion, nor am I a small contributor to the sound effects, with a running and reiterated apology for the amount of luggage and twice-and-more-told explanation that my tour takes me to such differing climates, I have to bring an en tout cas equipment. No one listens, everyone agrees, and somehow we move to a waiting car.

But a man seems to expect me to have luggage. I wonder why the women are always surprised. If I am a little apart from it, he points unerringly to the mound and says, "I expect those are yours," I agree, and feel no necessity for explanations about the climate. He picks up as much as he can carry, hands me the rest, and leads the way to his car.

In the car, however, whether man or woman-conducted, a topic of conversation which alarms me is invariably introduced. Am I sure I will be comfortable in the hotel? It's a pretty good hotel, they don't mind saying, for a town that size, but a hotel is never really like a home, is it? And Mrs. Somebody has said she would be delighted

to have me in her home, and I am not to think
that it would be a bit of trouble.

I am alarmed both because I know that I will
be a great deal of trouble to Mrs. Somebody if I
am to get my bags upstairs to the guest room,
let alone have my dress for the lecture pressed,
and because I may be coerced away from the hotel.
Here again, a man is easy. When I say that I
like hotels, he agrees with me, and promises to
square it with Mrs. Somebody. Women, however, and especially in groups, are strong, and
their pressure heavy. Many women, too, do not
like hotels, and count it brave to stay alone in a
strange one.

I know what an arrant coward I am about a
great many things—boats of any size from row
to liner; swimming in pool, lake or ocean; riding
on a horse, or in an automobile; walking across a
crowded street, or a field where there are cows;
and sitting anywhere where there are apt to be
wasps or bees. There are none of these potentials
in a hotel room. Therefore, to stay in one, requires no bravery from me. Furthermore, the fact
that "a hotel is never like a home, is it?" con-
stitutes for me, its greatest appeal.

A hotel room is an environment in which I

hum with contentment. I am surprised when people say too, that all hotel rooms look alike. No two of them look alike to me, and I have always an impatient anticipation when the bell-boy sets down my bags and inserts the key in the lock. My impulse is to step over the bags, push by him, and see quickly how this room looks. I do follow him with interest when he invites me to see the bathroom, the clothes closet, the light switch and the radiator valve. And then I am impatient for him to leave, so that I can get to the reading of all the printed announcements under the glass top of the bureau.

If, however, the bell-boy waves me into a room which is not made up, I am cross and unpleasant. The bell-boy is sorry—he telephones the clerk. The clerk explains how overcrowded and under-staffed the hotel is. I understand, but I am not mollified. I do not mind the disorder. I know that a chambermaid will fly through it on a broom, and make its surface immaculate. But someone has been sitting in my chair, someone has been sleeping in my bed, and I resent fiercely such intrusion, because one of the things I like best about a hotel bedroom is its lack of personal imprint. I view with astonishment and displeasure the women who boast of traveling always with their own pillows, couch throws, vases, and such knick-knacks. In no time at all, these monster snails say, they can give any hotel room the look of home. Why should they want to? Why must they carry their houses on their backs? The most charming quality of a hotel room for me, is its lack of resemblance to any home of my acquaintance.

I like my own house very much, but when I leave it, I want no reminders of it either with me or in the places where I shall temporarily "rest my wraps," a phrase I learned from New England hostesses. To be reminded of my own base makes me a little unhappy at having left it, and more than a little uncomfortable over the things in it that I have left undone. But to return to it from a round of dissimilar places is an unblemished pleasure. The wallpaper that is hanging in a fluttering strip in the guest room looks charming, and the dining room chair propped against the wall in lieu of the leg that has not yet been restored, is reassuring of things that do not change in a changing world.

In a hotel room there is seldom anything reminiscent of these dear souvenirs. In the presence of unhomelike surroundings and under the blessing of scholarly authority that we are all products of our environment, I become a very happy product. I revel in the minutiae which are no part of my home environment; for example, the "Do Not Disturb" sign with cord affixed for hanging on the door knob. Certainly, in my own simple way of life, I cannot hang a sign "Do Not Disturb" on my door knob. That is, I could hang it there, of course, but such a hanging would be observed about as seriously as the hieroglyphics chalked on my front door by Hallowe'en pranksters.

I do, in my own dwelling, every day, bawl down the back stairs that I would be grateful to be allowed to work without interruption. That is interpreted as an indication of wanting to be asked during the morning—have I anything to go to the cleaners? Do I wish to speak to the laundress about her private cleansing agent that burned large holes in the sheets last week and chewed out the monogram on a bath towel? Do I wish to have the turtle belonging to one of my twins, and inexplicably deceased, saved for her return from school, or disposed of? And who is home for dinner? But on the knob of a hotel bedroom door, "Do Not Disturb" is respected.

This is only one of the ways in which a hotel
indicates that it is yearning over me like a mother,
and I bask under such benevolent indulgence.
If I want a drink of cold water in the middle of
the night, I can have it brought to me. To satisfy
that whim at home I must go all the way downstairs, timorously pushing light switches on my
way, and fill a glass from the bottle in the ice
box, unless I am willing to settle for the tap in
the bathroom. But the tap in my bathroom is not
like other taps. At the instant of turning the
knob it releases a vigorous gush, icy cold, to the
amount of a little less than a quarter of a tumbler
full, and immediately after, a luke warm drizzle.
I do not know how long this continues before the
cold wave returns. I am too sleepy to wait it out.
I return to bed thoroughly chilled from the outside, and feeling inside as if I had refreshed myself by sticking my finger down my throat. There
are, of course, thermos jugs. Other people have
one beside the bed for just such needs. I have,
as a matter of fact, had one beside my own bed on
a tray, a glass beside it, just as the advertisement
pictures them, but I never, either by threat or
cajolery, succeeded in having it filled. To pour
from it each night, with eager, childlike hope,

and find it always empty, is to experience the torture of Tantalus. It is on the top shelf of the linen closet now, in the company of other disappointments—an appurtenance of the vacuum cleaner which was to purify the air by exhaling an aroma of pine needles, and came perilously close to asphyxiating the entire family, an electric croup bottle which spattered indelibly all the furniture and exposed bedclothing in the room, and a hair dryer which gave out shocks, and drew the hair into its coiled vitals.

The linen closet is the place, too, where our extra blankets and comforters are kept. A sudden turn in the weather at night poses the decision between a scuttle down the hall with the possibility that the added comforter will not restore you even to the level of warmth you are quitting, and a Laocoon arrangement of yourself in bed, which will allow you neither to return to real sleep the remainder of the night, nor emerge from that arrangement without pain, in the morning.

A hotel does not even allow such a problem to arise, and the way of avoiding it is very simple. The motherly management of a hotel places extra blankets in the bottom bureau drawer. It seems to me a charming place for them, but the bottom drawer in my bureau is filled with old pocketbooks. They are there because I have been intending, for several years, to sort out and give or throw away those of them over ten years old which have become out of style, or detached from the frames. If I relegated them to the linen closet, I would not get around to doing this.

From my Father, a winter-seasoned traveler, I learned an additional charm of the blanket in the hotel bureau drawer. The drawer is lined with newspapers, obviously of the town in which the hotel stands, and generally several months, sometimes some years, old. They make absorbing reading while waiting to be sleepy again.

The pleasure of ordering a pitcher of ice water in the night, pales beside the giddy delight of ordering food, any kind of food, at any hour. At home I know by ten o'clock in the morning what I am going to eat for lunch and dinner. I have reviewed what is in the ice box that can be used again with as little reminiscence as possible of the day before, and I have run, with Bill of the Fairlawn Market, the gamut of his suggestions. I furthermore know at exactly what hour I am going to partake of this set piece, and that if I am ten minutes out on my timing, I will eat under a lowering cloud of disapproval. But I have had, in a hotel, chocolate ice cream and ginger ale for dinner at midnight. I have not had it often. Actually, I have had it only once, and regretted the combination shortly after the having of it. Nevertheless, I ordered, and got it.

The taste of hotel food is not always to my liking, but its variety and its uncertainty are. Some hotels have given up dining room service since the war. Occasionally, the clerk forgets to mention this lapse until I have got into my wrapper and settled back against the pillow to order over the telephone a succulent tray. If I am plaintive enough, a bell-boy can be persuaded, sometimes, to fetch from the cafe up the street apiece, a hamburger, crisp french fried potatoes in a paper bag, and a bottle of milk. I can set these on the flat topped desk, draw up the one arm chair a hotel of that income bracket provides, put up my feet on the straight chair that "goes with" the desk, read a detective story, and eat, at any hour, and without talking to anybody. I consider this the Life Beautiful.

Sometimes the hotel uses discipline, as every mother must. It tells me to turn out the lights before leaving the room, put my jewelry in the safe downstairs——that always makes a fine joke between us, with some very snappy repartee from the desk clerk to me, and vice versa——and turn in my key at the desk.

One night I hurried to my room after a lecture to freshen up a bit before going on to a party. I left the key in the lock, and the house detective, seeing it as he passed by on his rounds, locked the door and put the key in his pocket. I discovered this when I telephoned the desk that I could not get out of my room. I discovered via the same channel that there was no duplicate key——"can't get new keys made now-a-days," that a master key was kept in the linen room, but the linen room was locked up, the bell captain had one, but he was off somewhere, and there wasn't a boy they could spare to chase after the house detective. I'd just have to wait till he turned in the key.

My friends, tired of driving around the block, came in to the desk, learned that I was being disciplined by the hotel truant officer, and organized a scouting party to round him up, each member covering a floor of the hotel. The scouts were so pleased by the opportunity to explore all its back lanes and passages, that I had been released for some time before they were gathered in again.

The detective was perfunctorily apologetic about my incarceration but genuinely suspicious of my carelessness. "A hotel tries to take care of its guests," he told the group sadly, "and then she goes and leaves a key hanging outside. It's an invitation to anybody." My friends assured him that the hotel was lucky to have a sharp man like him on the lookout for characters like me, and thanked him on behalf of the Chamber of Commerce. He was carried away by such fervent praise, and though a little doubtful of its sincerity, decided evidently to take no chances. When I returned from the party, he was in the lobby, and saw me to my room. I left at eight, the next morning. He was in the lobby when I came downstairs and saw me into the taxi.

I have been, I know, a trial to a hotel many times, but a hotel has failed me only once, and that time it was a deficiency of architecture, not personnel. Valets have pressed a lecture dress for me in such record time that I have put it on flinching from the heat it still carried from the steam iron. When I endeavored to do valets out of an honest fee by steaming dresses myself, suspended on hangers over a tub of hot water, the dresses fell more than once into the tub, and valets restored them. Chambermaids have got me into and out of recalcitrant zippers. Bell-boys have taught me to find the hideout of a shy radiator valve in any heating system, have sat on as many as five suitcases one at a time, to close them, and made into packages the remaining items which would not be included. The human element in a hotel has sustained me always. Its basic structure was the element that failed me once.

The hotel itself was pleasant. I came into it about ten o'clock at night, registered, gathered up accumulated mail, followed the bell-boy and my luggage to my room, learned from him the location of the bathroom, closet, light switches and radiator valve, and asked him to bring me some ginger ale. I changed from my traveling clothes to wrapper and slippers, and when the ginger ale came, settled down to enjoy it and the mail from home. Before I went to bed I did a little light washing and was put out to find that I had been given a bathroom with a shower, which I abominate, instead of a tub. It was too late, and I was too undressed to change, but there was no hanging space for the wash, not so much as a door to the shower over which to drape my pretties. They hung nicely, however, over bars of the coat hangers in the closet, and I went to bed.

The next morning I spoke my piece at ten in the auditorium of the local college, under the auspices of the Students' Literary Society. I went from there to a luncheon given by its officers, and presided over by a professor in the English Department.

The professor volunteered to see me back to my hotel, and in the car we talked about an article in the current Atlantic. I offered him my copy and he came up to my room for it, after he had parked the car. Standing in the middle of the room with the magazine rolled in his hand, he unexpectedly delivered a rather personal speech, emphasizing his remarks with the magazine, as if he were showing me his diploma. He was shorter than I, plumper, and, unless I give my own appearance far too much credit, considerably older. But his voice was so full of timbre that it jarred both of us, his phrasing magnificent, especially in the long dependent clauses, and his pauses fraught with significance. Between astonishment and inadequacy, I had no answer, other than a "no thank you," delivered in a reedy falsetto, which necessitated clearing my throat and saying it again.

Then I walked away and looked out the window, partly because I thought that would make getting away less awkward for him than if I watched him, and partly because that is what women on the stage and screen do.

Looking down at the street, though not very successfully, because the Venetian blind was down, I heard him walk heavily across the room, open the door and slam it. Simultaneously with my turning around, I heard a thrashing, tramping sound in the closet. The door of the closet opened violently and he burst out. He did not look at me, and I had nothing that seemed appropriate to say, but as he covered the four feet between the identical doors, opened the one into the hall with a force that very nearly took it from the hinges, and stormed through it, I saw, pasted down his back, three wet rayon stockings and a net brassiere.

Hotels ought to build the closet around the corner from the front door of a room.

The Evening Train

The road was winding and she had a tendency to accent on the accelerator, her vigorous conversation.

To go from my house to the village, I must pass under a Pennsylvania Railroad bridge, and I always stop at the approach to it. A Bryn Mawr boarding school and college tradition hangs heavy heavy over my head, that if you go under the bridge while a train is passing overhead, you will flunk your next exam. If you're caught unaware, however, holding a button will mitigate the curse. But the hold on me which is stronger than the curse, is the sight of the trains. I love to watch the fast ones go by me toward the West. They are going West when I see them, because I am not apt to be on hand as early in the morning as they come East. The ones I know best are the

Broadway, the General, and the Admiral. In the Autumn or Winter it is dark when they rush past me. Looking up, I see their lighted windows. I shall go home to a pleasant dinner—and for all my love of the Pennsylvania Railroad, I consider its food deplorable; but glimpsing the people at tables in the lighted dining car, I feel like the little match girl, and am choked with sorrow for myself.

Last November I took an unfamiliar train from Paoli to Harrisburg to reach a lecture engagement at Shamokin. As we left Paoli, I thought, with sudden pleasure that this particular stretch of track makes a bright thread which has run through my pattern for thirty-two years, and yet, traveling toward the West, I had not seen it by day, for a very long time.

There were so many of us who went home to the Middle West from college and boarding school, that the train, a powerful Express Limited, stopped at the tiny Bryn Mawr station just for us. We were always hysterically afraid that it would not stop, and always insufferably nonchalant for the benefit of the other passengers by the time it did stop. It reached us at about half past one in the afternoon. But the Chicago trains go later now, and they do not stop for me at Bryn Mawr. I take them at Paoli.

From that earlier train we watched the country-side closely in order to anticipate our arrival at Harrisburg. We had to be ready to spring out the moment it stopped, because tradition de-manded that we sprint up a steep flight of stairs from the tracks to the shed, buy a bag of hot pretzels from a man who sold them there and get back into the train before it pulled out. Immedi-ately it left the station, we ordered ginger ale, which was very sophisticated, to accompany the pretzels. The next and last tradition did not threaten us until we reached Pittsburgh. You couldn't go to bed until you had seen the Pitts-burgh girls off the train and all the way up the platform—and you had to run like a whippet to get back to the train in time. Now I go immedi-ately into the dining car for dinner, I do not get out at Harrisburg, and I am asleep long before we reach Pittsburgh.

The train I took to Harrisburg last November, left Paoli at one thirty-eight, almost exactly the minute we used to leave Bryn Mawr. That was why the bright thread ran through my memory so vividly. It went back even farther, to the first

time I rode over those tracks, long before boarding school. I went with my parents from Indiana
to Atlantic City to spend the summer when I was
five. Then I had raised the shade beside my berth
when I woke up—probably we had just left Harrisburg—and at my first sight of the gentle,
rolling Pennsylvania countryside, said that this
new country was "deeper than Indiana." The
phrase was repeated by my elders as a something
less than bright saying of the child, which is why
I am able to recall it. But I evidently thought that
the flat landscape of the Middle West, to which
I was accustomed, did not go down so far as these
Pennsylvania valleys and from that instant, I preferred the deeper country.

After that observation, I threw up. I remembered that, too, riding to Harrisburg, and that I
had been train sick most of the way. But it had
not dampened my love for trains, Pennsylvania
trains particularly, and though to this day, I have
to be wary about viewing the landscape from a
train window before breakfast, I always view this
particular one. I raise the shade beside my berth
as we pull away from Harrisburg, and feel my
heart leap up when I behold these hills and val-

leys, the loveliest in the world for me, particularly when I am riding on a Pennsylvania train.

This day in November, we came into Harrisburg at three o'clock. I climbed the stairs to the station. The man with the pretzels was not at the top. I realized for the first time, that in all the years I had never gone beyond the pretzel man. I had very little time now to explore the station, since I was making connections with a train for Sunbury, which left at three-twenty. I did stop at the news stand, because I saw pretzels for sale there.

The ride from Harrisburg to Sunbury was through unfamiliar country, along the Susquehanna river a good part of the way, and then up into the mountains. The trees were just past their full Autumn foliage, the reds, yellows and browns not so sharp as probably they had been a month before. Up the mountain side in masses they looked blurred, as if they had been smeared as I used to smear over all the color tablets in my tin Prang's paint box to see how they would look without dipping my brush in water between. We moved slowly, and made frequent stops. It was a very agreeable trip.

The station at Sunbury is sociably placed on

the corner of what looked to be one of the main streets of the town. I should have arrived at four-thirty but the train was late. It was five-thirty by the clock in the waiting room when I walked through to the street in search of a taxi, and the street was crowded with traffic. There were no taxis waiting. I did not see any sign indicating a cab stand so I set my bags on the curb and went back into the station to ask the ticket agent for help. He gave me a number to telephone and a cab arrived almost immediately. This was my first ride in a taxi equipped with a two way radio and the driver explained it. He was very pleased to show it off and said, too, that since the cabs had been equipped with these they did not hang around at the station but were on the go all the time and could be called in to the depot from anywhere for a passenger just as he had come for me. I had wondered, I told him, how he had got to me so quickly but, I said, the railroad station itself had seemed to be closer to the center of things than in most towns. He agreed with that and added that people found it very handy and that there was a lot of activity going on around the station. People seemed to like to stop by when a train was coming in. I said I could understand that and was telling him about how I always stopped at the bridge to see the Western trains go by, when we arrived at the Hotel Edison.

The chairman of the program for the evening came into the dining room while I was eating dinner, a little after seven. She said she would have some coffee and then we had better get started because we were to drive to Shamokin where the lecture was to be held at eight-fifteen. She told me, when I asked, that of course trains came into Shamokin, the evening train was an excellent one, but got in too late for my lecture. That was why we had to drive. She said that it was particularly important to-night for the lecture to start on time and that we ought to hurry. I had no opportunity to ask her the reason, because she went on immediately to tell me about the organization and Shamokin itself. But as we came out of the hotel, I said that I thought I had better admit immediately that I am idiotically nervous in a car and that I was extremely sorry we had to hurry. I confided too my preference for trains. She was understanding and indulgent, urging me as we started off to tell her whenever I thought we were going too fast. I did tell her several times because the road was winding and because she had a tendency to emphasize her vigorous conversation by pressing down on the accelerator. Apart from these disturbing spurts,—and she was as apologetic about them as I was about calling her attention to them—the ride was tolerable. She talked entertainingly, with a lively humor and was interested in a great many things.

The lecture was in a church but we went immediately up a flight of stairs to the second floor. I think the first floor was given over to Sunday school rooms and a sort of community house. Refreshments were to be served there later, I was told. Everyone seemed very pleased that we were on time. Again, I wondered about the necessity for it and why they seemed nervous. But I had no opportunity to ask and had also the impression that they were reluctant to talk about it.

I learned the reason immediately at the close of the lecture. The chairman announced that refreshments were to be served downstairs and asked the audience to move as quickly as possible without crowding. As I left the platform, she took my arm and said, just above a whisper, leaning toward me,

"I'll tell you now why we were so anxious about getting started on time. I didn't want to say anything about it earlier for fear it might up-set you. We had to be sure you'd get through before the evening train comes in because they're bringing back on it to-night the bodies of the boys from overseas. All the church bells in town are going to ring when the train comes in, and every-body has been asked to stand in silent prayer for three minutes."

A large clock hung on the railing of the gallery facing the platform. A woman near us looked up at it.

"The train's late to-night," she said. "It gen-erally is these last few years."

No one answered. The only sound was of our moving toward and down the stairs. Everyone was listening. As the chairman and I reached the top step, a woman half way down called back to me,

"You'll hear it whistle at the bridge. We al-ways time our getting down to the station that way."

She had hardly finished speaking when we all heard it. It whistled twice, one short and one long and thin, but heavy in the air. Two or three of us said simultaneously,

"It sounds like rain."

We smiled at one another, with quick mutual kinship, because we had all, in whatever town we had grown up, heard that kind of train whistle in the night, a whistle that lay heavy in the air, and as children heard our elders say,

"That means rain."

We moved on, listening. A woman one step below me turned to a friend on her left, and spoke so softly that I could not catch all the words,

"I can't seem to get Lon's boy out of my mind." I think Lon was the name. I am not sure.

"Is he on this train?" her friend asked, a little louder than the first, because she was startled. The first one nodded.

"He was always so crazy about trains, that evening train especially. He liked to see in the windows when it was lighted up. When he was little, he was always after his mother and father to take him down to the station to see it come in. I guess they're down there to-night. Everybody thought it would be better if they stayed home and waited, but I guess they're down there."

The bells began to ring.

In a Manner of Speaking

Ordinarily I do not make gestures.

SAINT NICHOLAS MAGAZINE once published a poem which I can still repeat. I had no reason then to question its sentiments. Now, however, some thirty years later, which is a very gentle approximation, I have a low opinion of its smug young hero. The poem began:

"Once there was a little boy whose name was Robert
 Reece.
And every Friday afternoon he had to speak a piece."

On the occasion which this poem records, Robert forgot his piece of that particular Friday afternoon. With an aplomb which at the time of my learning the poem, I considered magnificent, and now look upon as sickening, he substituted lines from the poems of preceding Fridays, and was very pleased with himself. The poem ends:

"You see it doesn't matter, Robert thought, what words
   I say,
 So long as I declaim with oratorical display."

After three seasons of lecture touring, I think I am qualified to assert that either Robert's oratorical display was certainly very handsome indeed, or Robert was a young squirt who did not know what he was talking about. I should like to tell that young man about an oratorical display of mine at DePauw University last season, which I would match against any of his, and I wish he could know what response I collected.

DePauw University is at Greencastle, Indiana. I have known about it always, but last winter was my first visit there. Like that Reece boy's, my piece (at DePauw) was on a Friday too; Friday morning, however, January sixteenth, at ten o'clock. The engagement before that was on the fourteenth of January in Winter Park, Florida, which seemed fairly remote from Greencastle, Indiana, until I got into conversation with the conductor on the train from Jacksonville to Cincinnati. I was to change at Cincinnati to a train to Greencastle.

The conversation grew out of the conductor's interest in my railroad ticket. My tickets for the entire tour are purchased by the lecture bureau, clipped together, and sent to me in a neat little folder. I am so afraid of tearing off the wrong ticket, or worse, the wrong half of a ticket, that I generally hand the whole sheaf to a conductor, and allow him to make his selection. Some conductors are bewildered by this display, but the gentleman on the Jacksonville to Cincinnati train was delighted by the sight. He lingered over the other tickets after extracting the one he required, leafed through them, and said,

"You're on a tour aren't you? Singer?"

I told him no, that I was a lecturer.

He was evidently disappointed by my calling, but polite. I understood his disappointment when he said,

"I used to be assigned to the Chicago Opera Company tours. There was a great bunch of people! The times we had on those tours. Never been anything like 'em since, I guess."

He told me a few episodes about them, and

certainly my own traveling by comparison, is hum drum.

As he talked, he was reading through my tickets again, and he broke off in the middle of an anecdote. He hadn't noticed, he said, the first time he looked through them, that I was going to Greencastle, and he wanted to know if by any chance I was speaking there at DePauw. I told him I was speaking there on Friday morning.

He handed back my folder and sat down in the seat facing me. He took a small notebook from his inside pocket, wrote something on one of its pages, tore the page out, and handed it across to me with the request that if I should happen to see the president of the university, I hand him that note. I told him I should be delighted to deliver it, and he sat back happily. He and the president, Claude Wildman, he was sure I knew his name, had been through High School together in Greensburg, Indiana. And the president's wife too, Forest, her name was, the prettiest girl in the class. "Smart as a whip, too," he added.

I settled back contentedly. This was good old familiar Hoosier talk, and I love it. I asked about the president. My friend the conductor—and we were friends by now, because we Hoosiers become friends with other Hoosiers quickly——my friend said that he had not seen the president for years, but at school he had been a great talker, a wonderful debater. Could talk on almost any subject extemporaneously. Had a fine vocabulary. He was, in fact, such a good talker, they had named him Demy. "Short for Demosthenes, you know." It was a pity I wasn't going to hear *him* make a speech.

I did not meet Dr. and Mrs. Wildman until Friday morning, although I arrived in Greencastle Thursday morning. A taxi was waiting for me, sent by the college to take me to Mason Hall. Mason Hall is a dormitory for girls; DePauw is co-educational. There are probably other girls' dormitories on the campus, but I did not leave my own until it was time to go to the lecture the following morning, because the weather was piercing cold.

Mason Hall is a beautiful new building, with the most attractive commons room that I have seen in any college. I was shown to the guest room on the first floor, and lunch on a tray was sent in to me. Shortly after, a group of girls called on me to ask if I would like to see the campus. I asked if they would mind very much my declining the invitation. They assured me that they would be delighted. The excursion had seemed to them a poor idea, but one that must be broached to visitors.

We settled down in the commons room to good talk, instead. Other girls joined us, coming in from classes. Some boys called on us too, later in the afternoon, and I had a thoroughly good time. I dined that night, and without having to go out. The dinner, at Mason Hall, was given by the girls' English, or perhaps Journalism Club, with their sponsor, a member of the English department, and one of the most delightful people I have met in a long time.

Immediately after early breakfast Friday morning, the president's secretary telephoned. The President was very sorry that he and Mrs. Wildman had not seen me yesterday, but they had been in Cincinnati at the conference of college presidents, returning late last night. They would both come over to Mason Hall, however, at 9:30 to take me to the lecture. Meantime the secretary had been instructed to ask me if she might take me over the campus. I declined. The weather had not changed.

The moment Dr. and Mrs. Wildman came toward me in the commons room I knew that I was going to like them. There was something about the way they called to me from the door, spontaneously and easily, which made me aware at once that they were warm, friendly, unassuming people, just the kind I would "fen for," if I were drawing up sides. We talked a little about the conference in Cincinnati, but Mrs. Wildman said it was time to start for the lecture. I suddenly remembered the message from my friend on the train, and took it from my purse. Dr. Wildman read it with delight, and passed it over to Mrs. Wildman. They both remembered their classmate, and were glad to hear from him after so many years. They had not seen him since High School days, but Dr. Wildman said they would certainly make a point of looking him up through the railroad, at Cincinnati.

As we left Mason Hall I asked if we had far to go. The weather was just as cold as I remembered from the day before. I learned for the first time, that I was speaking in a church—the Gobin memorial church—Dr. Wildman said, about a block away, and added that it was their only auditorium, but that they hoped some day to have another. I told him apprehensively that I was not sure that he knew that my lecture was not in any sense a church subject. Did he know that I was going to talk about Hollywood and motion pictures? He assured me that he did know. He had selected the subject himself. I need not be concerned, nor must I be put off by the incidental of speaking from the pulpit. It did put me off, however. I began to have misgivings about my being in Greencastle, Indiana, at all, in spite of my fondness up to this moment, for the people I had met there.

In the vestry, Dr. Wildman turned me over to a member of the English department, who was to introduce me. She told me that not only was I to speak from the pulpit, but I must speak into a microphone there, because the acoustics from that particular spot in the church were very faulty. I told her that I would be delighted to speak from any other spot. That was the only place, she said, from which I could be seen in the gallery. I protested that, born in the Middle West, I had a carrying voice, but she was firm. I dislike very much to use a microphone and told her so, but she repeated that there was no getting out of it.

She made the introduction from the chancel

steps while I sat in a high-backed chair behind her. At the conclusion of the introduction, she waved me to the pulpit. I had never stood actually in a pulpit before, and somehow to be there made me more nervous than I have been on any platform. It must have been my nervousness which made me forget the microphone. It may, of course, have been an inner obstinacy on my part. At any rate, I opened without it, and with the most curious effect I have ever experienced. My first few words rolled back to me from corners of the gallery, some time after I had spoken them, and was well into the next sentence. The result was a jumble of sound which certainly no one could have understood. It brought me around immediately, however, to remembering the microphone. And I could not find it. I looked over the pulpit, peered around it, tilted my head back to see if it could be dangling above me. It was not.

It was at this moment that the memory of Robert Reece came back to me. I had not thought of the boy for years, but the whole story came before me with dazzling clarity, and brought me inspiration. If Robert had accomplished triumph by oratorical display, in spite of confusion of words, I would give an oratorical display DePauw would long remember.

Ordinarily I do not make gestures, I think. At least what I did that morning felt very unfamiliar. I skipped a little, I pranced, I wreathed my arms around my head, stretched them toward the audience, flung them out from my shoulders as if I were doing setting up exercises, and I was contemplating one above my head, the other out from the shoulder, when I caught sight of the microphone. I am not surprised that I had not seen it before. I would not have thought of looking inside the pulpit, but it was imbedded there, beneath the hood, at a level with the flat surface of the desk top. Evidently it had been planned for the reading of the lesson or sermon.

In my relief at finding it, I discontinued my oratorical display abruptly. I put my face toward the little disc, and discovered that the regular occupant of the pulpit for whom the microphone must have been installed, was of proportions very unlike mine. The only way I could come within speaking distance of it was to lean well over the surface of the desk, and bend my knees. When I did this I disappeared immediately and completely from the sight of the audience. The position itself was difficult and uncomfortable to maintain. To ease the discomfort in my knees, I tried coming out around the side of the pulpit, being careful to accompany each sally with strong gestures. I came out, too, because I felt an urgent necessity to re-establish communication with my audience, in order to see how we were getting on together. I am accustomed, when I speak, to watch the audience carefully. If I see—and it is very easy to see—that its temper is being tried by too long an exposition, I hurry to an anecdote. I have felt, too, an obligation to be visible. If I am engaged to appear before an audience, it has seemed to me that I ought to appear. But when I appeared skittishly around the pulpit at De-Pauw, interpreting the jumble of my words by sprightly pantomime, I had the uneasy impression that my audience was not happy to have me there. Accordingly, after perhaps three sorties, I retired behind the pulpit to stay, bent my knees, and maintained that position for the remaining fifty minutes of my allotted hour.

The speech finished, I came out for the last time from behind the pulpit to make my bow to the audience, and discovered that after fifty minutes of bending, I was unable to straighten my knees. The very effort to straighten them so intensified the cramp in my muscles, that I gave a sudden leer from excruciating pain. From the moment of my arrival in the town, I had loved the people there. Now I wanted only to get away from them all as quickly as possible. My exit, however, was not quick. Bent and cramped, I shuffled slowly off the stage. With the purpose of distracting attention from my posture, I accompanied my departure by a final flight of pantomime in as many gestures of farewell as I could conjure up during my passage.

I did not return for a second bow. I was in no position for it, but as I sat in the ante room, rubbing my knees, a woman approached me.

"I wanted to tell you, Miss Kimbrough," she said with certain emphasis, "that we enjoyed *what we heard* this morning very much."

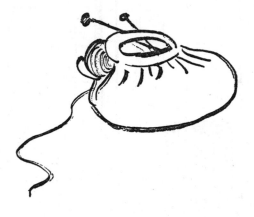

No Friends or Relations

"*. . . at least I won't be able to look at you.*"

THE FRIENDS OF MINE whose profession involves making public appearances, and who plead annihilating nervousness before each one of them, receive small sympathy from me. They should have considered that factor, I not only think but tell them, before adopting such a career. Or, if they had not anticipated this anguish, changed to another field, once they found they were victims of it. There are a number of lines of work, I have pointed out, which exact little contact with people at all, either publicly or privately—naturalists who live in solitude and send out their findings from the forest depths, forest rangers, lighthouse keepers, weather reporters, who live on mountain tops. Raising bees, I am told is an un-social occupation. There are many livelihoods, I am sure, which could not possibly involve a public appearance, and I recommend their investigation by all my friends who suffer from stage fright.

If I seem unfeeling about this, it is because I have heard so many times, the performer engulfed backstage with words of praise for the performance, and cries of pity for the strain and terror of doing it. Never a word nor glance of sympathy to those friends of the artist who, along with me, are leaning haggard against a wall of his dressing room, because our knees are too weak to sustain us un-aided. Our hands are cold and clammy. We have suffered two hours of such excessive perspiration that we are dehydrated. We have digested nothing of the meal which preceded the performance, and it lies heavy in us. We would have given anything and all we had to have changed places with our friend, the performer. Not that we would have been capable of giving the performance, nor even in our pitiable condition have been so mentally distraught as to think we could, but at least we would have been afforded the opportunity to do something—to be up there on the stage fighting——instead of sitting helpless and ague-ridden.

In this, perhaps, unfeeling point of view, I am at least consistent, I think, because when the conditions are reversed, and I am actually the one on the platform, my heart goes out to the friends and family below me in the audience. I know what they are suffering, and their presence induces in me the very distress for which I have berated my performing friends. The difference is, however, that with them it is chronic, whereas I suffer this acute nervousness only in the presence of family and friends. If they could be eliminated from audiences, the stage and lecture platforms would be happier places for everybody. I would rather, I think, attempt a concerto before strangers——and I never in my fullest musical flowering progressed beyond MacDowell's Water Lilies—— than speak a piece I know before my dear ones.

The behavior of these dear ones in the audience does not tend to ameliorate my nervousness. Certainly it emphasizes their own. They hold, moreover, my riveted attention with the same horrid fascination that the telegraph pole exacts from a beginner on a bicycle. Early and painfully acquired experience has taught me that the members of my family are not silent spectators. They were the forerunners of the audience participation programs. I was never in a school play that I did not receive instructions from my mother in the audience, delivered in what might technically be known as a whisper, but had the carrying power of a church bell.

My first exposure to an audience in recent years, was at a program of Information Please. And the audience included members of my family. My stability on that occasion, both nervous and mental, was as the stability of a bowl of Jello. I had put to myself and received no comfort from them, the questions by which I have sought to comfort friends about to give a performance. "Why was I there?" "Had anyone forced me to go on the program?" "Of all the things I might be doing on that evening, why had I selected this occupation?" And though I reminded myself that I was going to be paid for it, which is, for me, the strongest incentive to any kind of work; on this occasion, it brought me no comfort. Mr. Dan Golenpaul, the kindly owner and instigator of the program, had taken me out to dinner on that evening. It is his custom, I believe, with Information Please novices—

at least he did not repeat the ceremony the second time I went on the program. But on that first night, at dinner, he coached me soothingly. The important thing was, he said, to speak up, and I must not mind if my answer was wrong. They loved sending out Encyclopedia Britannicas, he assured me, and fifty dollar bonds. The only thing that distressed him and his colleagues, was silence. I must laugh, sing, make myself audible in some way to the listening audience.

When he had administered the amount of steak and lofty sentiment he felt sufficient to carry me through the evening, he took me to the broadcasting studio, where he transferred my dead weight from his arm to a chair on the stage behind a table on which a microphone had been placed. Mr. Frank Adams was seated on my left, Mr. John Kieran on my right. And two nobler, prettier souls are not to be met anywhere. They nodded and smiled at me, they even patted my palsied hand, and swore a solemn oath that when the program ended I would still be alive.

Mr. Fadiman, behind a table on the opposite side of the stage, was able, by waving, to direct my focus to him, and explained some technicalities, I think, though a roaring in my ears caused my hearing to be defective, too. I gathered, however, that we were to have a warm up question and answer period for ten minutes before we went on the air, so that by the time the program actually began we would all be having fun. There was laughter at this from the audience already assembled in the studio, and I managed a polite bray. I took a quick look at the audience. It seemed a good time to do it while my vision was blurred, though I had no reason to think, from the way I felt, that it would ever clear again. Out of the mist, however, rose instantly the faces of my brother and sister-in-law, and from the expression on them I had a dismal idea of the way I looked.

Mr. Fadiman rapped on the table to call the troupe and the audience to order, and proposed the first question. I like to remember that in the warm-up period, I was very close to spectacular. There were very few questions I could not answer, although I admit grudgingly that Mr. Fadiman has a talent for extracting from me far more than I have ever known. I do not like to remember, however, that the moment the signal was given that we were on the air, a kind of paralysis settled over me, which caused me to mutter to myself,

"You know your name and where you live. Just hold on to that."

The paralysis extended also to the muscles of my jaw in a mysterious fashion so that when I did essay an answer to the question,

"Name an article of apparel, or an accessory worn today, which our grandmothers wore," I endeavored to say "a snood." I pronounced it "a snud."

Mr. Fadiman did not understand me, and I can scarcely wonder at it, but when he asked me to explain what I had said, my power of speech dried up altogether, and I could only point piteously to that very accessory which I myself was wearing to bind up my hair.

Things got a little better after that. At least, I was able to give an appreciative whinny or two, to an answer from Mr. Adams or Mr. Kieran, in order to let the listening audience know I was there, and later on even worked up to a few answers myself, though not very good ones.

"Now," said Mr. Fadiman, "we'll have a go at a musical question. Identify the source of the music which depicts children dreaming of angels mounting a ladder to heaven."

I was thinking. So were Mr. Adams and Mr.

Kieran, when we all, including Mr. Fadiman and the audience, heard a deep groan, as of someone in great pain. I had no need to look I knew it was my brother. I did look, however, and was transfixed.

My brother and sister-in-law were mouthing something at me, accompanying their grimaces by as spell-binding a piece of pantomime as I have ever watched. They clasped their hands, rolled their eyes up to heaven, simpered, wiggled their shoulders, unclasped their hands to make signs of something going up in the air, something which had cross pieces on it. And all the time, with eyes starting out, they mouthed. Of course it was against the rules. Mr. Fadiman had asked particularly at the opening of the program, that the audience give no help, but Mr. Fadiman need have felt no concern over the help I was getting from this exhibition. The only thing it did was to throw an hypnotic spell over me, so that I was totally unable to drag my attention away. I sat in absorbed and dreamy contemplation of the act until the clang of the cash register and the announcement that a set of the Encyclopedia was on its way to Mrs. Somebody brought my bemused senses back to Mr. Fadiman and the next question.

At the conclusion of the program I learned that my brother and sister-in-law had been under the impression that they were revealing to me the Children's Prayer from Hansel and Gretel. That particular selection happens to be the first song I was ever taught to sing, and I learned it at the age of three or thereabouts. I do not say that merely by reason of having known it most of my life I would have remembered it on Information Please, but I do maintain that with such family assistance and participation as were given me that night, the song would never have come remotely near my memory.

My friends, too, though less audible than my family, have diverse ways of making their presence in an audience to which I am speaking, constantly known to me. One of these, a very dear friend, volunteered to motor with me to my first lecture engagement of the season this year. The lecture was to be in New Jersey, not a hundred miles from where I live. On the way, by some ill chance, I ventured to say that I was particularly nervous about this engagement because it was the first of the season. After the second or third, I told her, I felt at ease, but the first one, after the long break of the Summer, was an engagement I dreaded. I was merely making conversation. Nothing that she could answer would be of any comfort to me, but I was startled by the anger my observation provoked.

Why had I not told her this earlier, she demanded. Had she had any inkling of the way I felt, nothing would have induced her to be a witness to the performance. I ought to know how nerve-wracking it was anyway for her to listen to me.

I assured her humbly that indeed I did know. I had been in her position many more times than in the one I was about to take, and that there could be no comparison between her discomfort and mine. My sympathy mollified her a little. And, she added, thank goodness she had brought her knitting. She could concentrate on that. It would provide a therapy.

I was surprised because, as well as I know her, I had never seen her knit. She had not done any knitting for several years, she admitted, but something had prompted her to go to the attic that morning before leaving, and pull out from a trunk, a knitting bag she remembered putting away two or three years before, with a half-finished scarf in it, together with the wool and needles. She indicated it on the seat beside her.

"I'll have such a hard time remembering how to knit," she said, "that at least I won't be able to look at you."

I agreed that this would be the most satisfactory way to treat the lecture, and she was reconciled to the prospect.

At the club house of the ladies' organization sponsoring the lecture, the chairman immediately took charge of my friend, leading her, while I waited in the vestibule, to a seat near the front. Returning to me, she said that she would occupy the seat next her after she had introduced me. We came up the aisle together and I preceded her, as she had instructed, up the steps and onto the stage. I took a seat behind the lectern while she made a few opening announcements and then introduced me. I stepped to the lectern. The chairman, after a bow to me and the audience, left the platform, and I watched her settle down in the seat beside my friend, before I began to speak.

Because of my magnetic though reluctant attraction to family or friends in the audience, and because I knew exactly where this friend was sitting, I could not keep my attention from her. With an effort which came near to distracting me completely from what I was saying, I would pull away from her to look out over the remainder of the audience. In a few sentences I would find myself staring at her again.

I saw her take her knitting from the bag, after a quick and resentful glance at me. When I came back to her again, the sight I saw enchanted me to a fixed stare from which I never deviated during the remainder of the lecture. She was knitting from tiny strands of wool, each of them no longer than an inch, which she tied painstakingly together first, and then knitted over the knots. She never looked at me again, and I never looked away from her. Neither did the chairman, nor the members of the audience within a radius of several rows across the aisle from her.

At the conclusion of the lecture, the chairman met me at the foot of the steps from the platform. She was polite about my piece, but her thoughts were elsewhere, and after a scant and perfunctory three or four sentences about my part in the program, she revealed eagerly where they were. Could I, she wondered, explain about my friend's knitting. It had seemed to her so unusual. She did not recognise the pattern. She was sure she had never seen one like it before, and she could not quite figure how it was going to come out. I told her it was not one with which I was familiar either, and that I too had been most interested in it. The chairman added that several other members had inquired about it.

On my way home, I told my friend of the chairman's interest. My friend said she was not surprised. She didn't suppose any of them had seen a pattern like that before, because she had found, when she took the wool from the bag, that the moths had got in it, and chewed it into tiny pieces. So she had just tied the fragments together, and kept going.

"Otherwise," she added reproachfully, "I would have had to listen."

With Milk and Honey

The girls at the sorority house were sympathetic to my crusade.

THE BUS LEFT from Corvallis at 9:55 and so I had time that morning to drive around the campus of Oregon State College before going to the station. I had arrived the morning before at 11:15 by bus from Albany, and spoken that night, but the day had been so filled with a round of festivities, there had been no time for a tour. We had begun with a luncheon at one of the sorority houses. Remembering the bleak parlors at the dormitories in which I had lived at my own college, I looked with astonishment at the luxury and taste of the furnishings of the sorority house and felt very far away from my own Bryn Mawr, Pennsylvania. The twenty, or perhaps, thirty girls were attractive looking, more neatly dressed, too, than those on my college heath, and they simmered with enthusiasm.

I talked with them after lunch about the careers to which they aspired, and when some of them spoke timidly of further college work in the East, I gathered up shield and spear, and flung myself into the crusade I follow, for education away from home. Ever since I started lecture touring, I have been disturbed by the sectional boundaries in this country which the young do not cross. Most of those who go to college, go to one in their own state and tend, I think, to have an uneasy suspicion of undergraduates, or graduates for that matter, from other parts of the country. I thought it would be a wonderful thing, I told these girls, if there could be an exchange of students among colleges in this country as there is an exchange of students between the United States and Europe. I, myself, I said, born and brought up in the middle West, had gone East to college and been happy at the combination. I would like to see students from Maine or Massachusetts go to Illinois or Wisconsin, and students from Wyoming or Idaho take their junior year in Ohio, Rhode Island or Connecticut.

I was not sure that they would agree with me. I had proposed the idea one evening at dinner to the president of a college in Ohio and he was horrified. The increase of students since the war under the G.I. Bill was so great, he explained, that they had even had to restrict their candidates to those not only living in Ohio but born there. They had, as a matter of fact, he said, tried to dispose of some of their overflow to Colorado, but Colorado would have none of them.

The girls at the sorority house were sympathetic to my crusade. Several of them flattered me by saying that though they had not thought about it particularly before, after hearing me, they believed they would see if they could take at least one semester in an eastern institution. I congratulated them enthusiastically, but I was a little taken aback when they cited as their preference for this experiment, the University of Colorado. I accepted it, however, as a short step in the right direction.

Later that afternoon there was a large tea at another of the sorority houses, and I was impressed by the luxury and charm of its furnishings, too. I dined before the lecture with members of the faculty. We had good talk, but reviewing it later that night as I went to bed, I realized that we had not touched on any of the topics which, in a group of that sort in the East, would invariably have been mentioned, such as current plays, musical events, or even the anecdotes going the rounds at home. That may have been because I was asking questions about the college and its activities, but I did remember too that when we got onto politics, it was from a sectional rather than an international, or even national, approach, with the emphasis on how their lumber and canning industries were affected.

One of the group suggested the tour of the college next morning before the bus left and he called for me at half past eight. It was the second of December, but the weather was only cool and moist. The campus was green and beautiful. My guide told me that it covered, together with the experimental farm, nearly six hundred acres and that there were nearly a thousand acres in addition, not part of the campus proper, but used by the college, plus 75 thousand acres of State forest under the college management. In addition to these, the agricultural department maintained about two thousand acres under its own supervision.

When I was a little girl, I had told him, an aunt of mine had come out to Corvallis from Columbia University to teach home economics in this very college, and that in the family we had always called her the "pioneer." I was sure, I told him, that somewhere I still have a picture postcard album filled with the cards she sent from Oregon, and I treasured them with the same reverence paid those from Mrs. Eva Little who lived a block away from us in Muncie, Indiana, and went out to Africa on a trip with a missionary from the Presbyterian Church. Now that I saw the place and learned the area it included and the scope it covered, I felt my reverent approach to the postcards had been quite right. My aunt, a widow, had taken with her her son, Charles Robbins, my cousin, who is four years older than I. For a long time after that, one wall of my bedroom was covered by a banner the size of a bedspread which bore in orange felt the letters, "O A C." The fact that he actually lived at Oregon Agricultural College, gave him a larger than life importance, a fact which he reiterated in each communication to me and which I found both awesome and exasperating. I had never dreamed, somehow, that one day I would actually see Corvallis, Oregon, and the Oregon Agricultural College, that "O A C" of my childhood. The span from home to Europe had not seemed so broad as this. My guide was understanding. He had felt exactly like that, he told me, when he first came out, and it was interesting, too, to discover that most of the members of the faculty had "come out" from some other part of the country. When he told me, too, that the most popular courses, apart from agriculture, were logging engineering, lumber manufacture and commercial canning, the distance from home seemed even greater than before.

I was thinking of all this when I said goodbye to him at the station and climbed into the waiting bus. There were not more than a dozen passengers, and I was a little surprised when an old lady sat down beside me, because there were plenty of vacant seats. I did not mind, I only noticed it. I was reviewing in my mind the things I had seen and heard, and wondering how, in spite of its beauty, the people who had come there to teach from other parts of the country, had adjusted themselves to this remoteness from the things they must have known. I had said, when they asked me, that I lived outside Philadelphia, and that one of the things I liked best about it was that I could live in real country and yet be easily accessible, both to the city of Philadelphia and to New York. They had agreed with me and I wondered now if they had not been a little wistful about it. It was all very well to know that an aeroplane could take you back to New York within a few hours, but I doubted that many of them, any more than I, could afford to take a plane on an impulse to see a play, as I can take a train that runs every hour from Philadelphia.

Probably these people came to Portland, or perhaps down to San Francisco, the most exciting city, I think, in this country. But from the way the students had pummeled me with questions, I doubted that their radius of travel around Corvallis was very wide. They did, of course, have a wonderful outdoor life, and were undoubtedly blessed with great self-sufficiency. They must have made their own entertainment always. As children their Saturday treats certainly could not have included trips to museums, concerts, opera, theaters and Schwarz's, or Wanamaker's or Marshall Field's. Their lives were far from barren, but I would not call them altogether rich.

The old lady beside me said, "This your first time out here?"

I had been aware of her so absentmindedly, I had not realized, until I turned to answer, that I must have noticed only her hands when she sat down. They were old from work, and so was her figure, but her face was shining and vigorous. I told her this was my first visit to Oregon. She nodded happily.

"I thought so," she answered, "that's why I decided to sit down here beside you. I like to talk about it. You don't mind, do you?" she added politely.

I told her I did not mind in the least and that I thought the country beautiful. I would like to hear everything I could about it. She leaned against the back of the seat and looked past me out the window. From that moment I think she did not talk to me, and that very soon she forgot I was there. I think she only wanted to say aloud these things. She said them without emphasis, but without pauses, too. I think she had said them to herself so many times that they had become a song. This is her Plain Song:

"I grew up on a farm in Iowa. We grew good corn, but the work was hard. Autumn was pretty though, when the corn was high, and July too, when you could hear it growing. I didn't marry until I was twenty-five. My husband was a farmer, too, but the grasshopper plague hit us, took everything we had. My husband was so discouraged, he didn't want to try again, so we moved to Kansas. We were doing all right there, but the work was hard, and then the dust storms hit us. After that, we moved to Oklahoma. I don't like to remember that time—we nearly starved to death. I don't know how we ever got enough together to move out, but somehow we did, and we came to Oregon. My husband took a job in a mill and I worked too, until we could buy ourselves a little place. Not far from Albany it is, about twenty miles from here.

"The first summer we were in it I canned everything I could lay my hands on. As soon as it come up I was digging it and canning it. I liked to have died, I stood over that stove so much that summer, but I vowed we wouldn't be so hungry again as we'd been back there. And it wasn't for a year that I knew for sure we'd not starve here. A person couldn't.

"I couldn't seem to take it in at first, but I had most of the stuff left over from my canning because I didn't need it. Fresh stuff coming along all the time, and plenty of it. And flowers. The flowers I've got. Never had time for them back there, the work was so hard. I never could seem to make them grow anyway. But out here! I don't do much fussing over them. Oh, a little, because I'm so fond of them, but they grow anyhow. Roses! I've got some blooming right now, big as my hand. Some are little pink ones, red, white—I got all kinds. I don't think I could ever have enough of them. When we first come out here I used to dream sometimes that we'd gone back to those other places. My husband would have to shake me awake because he said I was crying out loud in my sleep and I could feel, after he woke me up, how my face and the pillow were all wet from me crying. But I haven't had that dream in a long time.

"I guess maybe I'm getting lazy now, and my husband. We used to be good workers, too, but now it seems as if we just like to sit on our front porch and watch our things growing. He bought me a rocking chair. We sit there and watch and I rock, and rock and look."

I thought she had finished. She looked down at her hands, opening her fingers and examining the palms, then the backs. She folded her hands, looked out the window again, and told another verse.

"I never thought I'd see a land with milk and honey blest. Not while I was living, anyway. But I'm living in it every day, every single day. The wonder of it. The wonder of it."

She was looking out the window and she began to sing, not loud, and yet enough for the people in the seats ahead to recognize the tune and to join in. The people ahead picked it up and those behind us, all down the length of the bus. She did not wait for us, but when she had reached the last line, we were all singing, the bus driver the strongest of all, nodding his head to keep us in time. We were all together at the second round, and though we didn't know all the words, we sang it through from beginning to end, the old, brave hymn,

Jerusalem the golden!
　With milk and honey blest;
Beneath they contemplation
　Sink heart and voice opprest.
I know not, O I know not,
　What joys await us there!
What radiancy of glory!
　What bliss beyond compare!

．　．　．　．　．　．　．　．

O sweet and blessed country,
　The home of God's elect!
O sweet and blessed county,
　That eager hearts expect!
Jesus, in mercy bring us
　To that dear land of rest!
Who are, with God the Father,
　And Spirit, ever blest. Amen

It's the Hospitality

The offering startled me.

ALONG ABOUT the third week of a lecture tour I begin to feel an ominous tightening, a constriction. I pretend, at first, that this is not so. I am being foolishly nervous and apprehensive, I tell myself. When the sleeves of my dress seem uncomfortably binding around the arm holes, I say promptly that cleaners are shrinking clothes just as successfully now as they did during the war. But on the day when I include a piece of my waist in the run of the zipper on my girdle, I know that my imagination has not caused this pain, nor have cleaning establishments. The thing I have dreaded has come—weight. I am being fattened by kindness; the kind hospitality of the ladies who sponsor my lectures, because I am an object of hospitality.

If, on a lecture tour, I could not only stay, but eat at a hotel, I could at least maintain my middle-aged proportions. In a hotel, I order food sent to my room so that I will not be tempted by the asparagus with Hollandaise at the next table, nor the cart of French pastries wheeled up by the waiter with persuasion and within easy snatching. I squeeze a wretched grapefruit instead, but I can only do it when I am locked in my own room. Let me so much as go downstairs, and I weaken. Let me step from the hotel into the plump hands of the hospitality committee, the zipper on my girdle inevitably will catch me. And it always does.

The hospitality committee catches me actually, even before the lecture tour begins. From the moment the contract is signed, the ladies are lying in wait for me, but not secretly. They state their purpose flatly in the contract. These contracts between lecture bureau and organization are printed on a leaflet the size of a sheet of type-writing paper folded lengthwise and each organization which "has me" has also, of course, a separate contract. About a week before I start on the tour, the lecture bureau mails to me the accumulated sheets. They are closely printed on both sides, and the first season on receiving them, I read every printed word, pondering over the fact that W. Colsten Leigh, Inc., 521 Fifth Avenue, New York, N. Y., was hereinafter to be referred to as the "Bureau Party of the first part," while the specific organization concerned was hereinafter to be referred to as the "Sponsor Party of the second part. Such handsome wordage evidently confused me into the subconscious impression that a new political system was being established, because more than once that autumn I dreamed that I was at the polls and could not make up my mind whether to vote Bureau or Sponsor. More than my subconscious mind, however, was affected and is still affected by the phrase that follows: "In consideration of the mutual and dependent covenant hereinafter set forth, the sponsor engages and the bureau shall *furnish*," and at this point there is inserted in typewritten, capital letters, "EMILY KIMBROUGH."

Emily Kimbrough to be furnished is a disturbing statement to read. What temerity on the part of the Bureau Party to offer me as a furnishing to anyone, and what am I thinking of to allow

my inadequacy to be so exposed! I am uncomfortably enough aware of my inadequacy in the
comparatively unexposed speaking activities in my
life, telling the painter what color I want, or
knowing myself, telling garage men the number
of pounds of air I want in the tires or the number
of the oil I use. Yet all these inadequacies pale
beside my contemplation of Emily Kimbrough
publicly furnished to anyone.

In my experience, there is only one other invitation to inadequacy so complete. That is in
Hollywood at what is known in some circles there
as a "premeer," the gala opening of a motion picture, with grandstands set up on either side of the
theater, and packed with eager fans; white and
colored floodlights sweeping across the front of the
theater like a blinding rain, then flashing up
across the sky. Each of these lights is as big as a
baby Austin. They are mounted on trucks lined
up in the street facing the theater, and are operated from their own generators which give out a
permeating, humming sound. People are so
thickly planted on the sidewalks that they bulge
out over the street and are tied back like rambler
roses by a line of policemen along the curb. Radio
men stand on a platform set up beside the box

office and whisper into a microphone what comes out in a blare of super tremendous adjectives describing the event. Within an area of a quarter of a mile, only the automobiles boasting an invitation sticker pasted on the windshield are admitted. These cars drop into line and into first speed to lurch along up to the door where they are relieved of their passengers and driven off by princes and noblemen of old St. Petersburg or Vienna, perhaps, in glittering uniforms with white capes. As each automobile approaches, the fans on the sidewalk and in the grandstand identify its occupants, screaming with exultation the news of their approach. "It's Clark Gable and Anita Colby," they tell the world, cheering them and their own announcement with happy yells. "It's Rex Harrison and Lilli Palmer—They're *married*." "It's Ray Milland and the Mrs." The crowd is hysterically grateful that the Millands have left their own fireside. "It's nice they came," women in the crowd call to one another and wave to them understandingly as if sharing a bond of unwashed supper dishes and mending to be done because they are all out on a spree. "Here's Betty Hutton." And as Betty descends from the car, "How's the baby, Betty? Give us a look at your husband. Turn around—let's see how the back of your dress is made." And she does. I am in that line lurching along in first speed driving my Oldsmobile of 1939 or '40—I can never remember which—and when the crowd sees it, it bellows forth the announcement. Up and down, back and forth, across the grandstand, down the sidewalks and into the foyer, it yells the news of my coming.

"It's nobody" rings out the cry and when it has been taken up, distributed throughout the waiting crowd, there is silence. That is the deadest moment in the low tide of inadequacy that I know. But there is a difference of only a very few minutes between it and the contemplation of Emily Kimbrough furnished.

As a furnishing, I brood to myself, how do they know that I will be any more compatible to their background than the chairs furnished to my living room for my Christmas carol party by Mr. Moody, our village undertaker? Mr. Moody, however, sends his furnishing to me free. My Bureau Party does not send me free to the sponsors, nor can I be sent out on approval. They have me, and that is all there is to it. Not quite, as a matter of fact, because they must also, according to the closely printed contract which I used to read so carefully, "furnish a well heated, lighted, and licensed place for me, in good condition,"—I doubt if my living room does as well for Mr. Moody's chairs—"and, if necessary, a stereopticon or motion picture machine with both licensed and experienced operators." That is a provision I wish I could claim. There is nothing I should like better than a stereopticon or motion picture machine and an experienced operator, together with some good slides or film. Then we could all sit down and enjoy the evening. But I am a solitary furnishing without benefit of any of these pleasant accessories. And the Sponsor Party must "have me."

The Sponsor Party is sturdy and courageous. It does not take its furnishings lying down. It does not even wait for them. It advances to meet them in a solid flank of hospitality and with notice in the contract of its coming. This is the only part of the contract I read now when the batch arrives. I ignore all the printing that tells of the Bureau and Sponsor Party. I turn quickly away from who and what are to be furnished. I am for the typewritten messages in the spaces between that will tell me what kind of a party the Sponsor

Party is throwing up as brave defense against the coming Kimbrough. MISS KIMBROUGH, they say, WILL BE MET BY THE RECEPTION COMMITTEE AND WILL LUNCH WITH THE ORGANIZATION PRECEDING THE LECTURE. If the lecture is at night, dinner is stipulated instead of lunch. And, the contract continues, "Formal Evening Dress requested," or "Day Dress" or "Formal Afternoon Dress."

In their very effort to be fair and square, however, they rout me, because I do not know exactly what a formal afternoon dress is. I have never outgrown the category by which my wardrobe was designated when I lived in Muncie, Indiana, and we moved away from there when I was twelve. In Muncie I had a party dress, a Sunday school dress, school dress and a play dress. Summertime called for special equipment, but for the greater part of the year, a play dress was actually a wilted school dress. So the major discriminations were party, Sunday school and school. I translate them today as evening dress; church, town, or daytime lecture dress; and going-to-market or working-at-home dress. Those are definitions which I understand and I buy my clothes accordingly. A formal afternoon dress has never swum into my ken. The only period in my life when I was formal in the afternoon was on Saturdays during my years at college when I met a beau at the Bellevue-Stratford or under the clock at the Biltmore and we attended a thé dansant. I have not been to one of those for some time.

Once I am with the Sponsor Party, however, at their party, whatever time of day, my uneasiness over the accuracy of my apparel will disappear, because enjoyment of people is indigenous to me, as it is, I think, to all Hoosiers—and a few other people. I will, therefore, have a good time with them—save for one other aspect which I dread. The Sponsor Party itself may be apprehensive, or it may be brave about the coming Kimbrough furnishing. It may conceivably be piercingly bored. Kimbrough is just one more in the long line of furnishings, season after season, to be met, listened to, and fed. And in the specific vocabulary of the Sponsor Party, the visiting furnishing is always listened to. Just as the members of an organization always speak of "having" Sinclair Lewis, or Cornelia Otis Skinner, whoever it may be, so they "hear" whoever is appearing before them. "We heard Angna Enters last season," they will say, and this seems odd because the particular genius of Miss Enters lies in her ability to convey so much without uttering a word. They do hear me—I am that kind of furnishing. But, oh, they do not have to feed me. It is this aspect that I dread. It is the only real obstacle to my Hoosier enjoyment of any and all Sponsor parties. If only they would extend the hand of hospitality and let me grasp it instead of taking from it a plate of chicken salad, hot buttered rolls, green peas and jelly, knowing that in the end, my girdle will find me way out.

I do not understand why it is that a woman alone will eat something out of the icebox for lunch, but in a group of more than two, must provide for herself and for them something of mayonnaise or cream or both. A man's idea of a hospitable meal is a good steak and I happen to consider that one of the finest ideas in the world. Incidental to its own excellence it is also recommended on the diet that I follow. The fact that this particular diet is sponsored and recommended by Mr. Clark Gable is not entirely incidental to my reason for following it. I do not mean that he personally drew it up for me, but his name and photograph headed the article which I cut out of the Sunday newspaper. And he said steak or a chop as a mainstay. That is, alas, masculine mainstaying. A woman's idea of a hospitable meal under group thinking is a chicken patty with peas, and when I am out on the chicken patty circuit, my figure goes the way of all flesh, to my hips.

I know that there are those who return from the chicken patty circuit unspread. But they are the fortunate ones who are too nervous to be able to eat anything before a lecture or a performance. I am nervous too, but my nervousness is not so refined. It always makes me extremely hungry. When at separate times each of my twins had her appendix out, I ate almost unceasingly for several days and was in a very bad shape long after the twin was fully restored to health. And so, at a group meal, before a lecture, I eat my own roll and those of my neighbors in addition to my chicken patty and ice cream. If I were in a hotel, I would not allow myself to order such things and I would be neither more nor less nervous on a piece of steak and lettuce without dressing.

I wish, too, that the social functions, whatever the food, could be given *after* the "hearing" instead of just *before* a job to be done. Then I could really give myself up to the good old Hoosier enjoyment of meeting people, without being nervous and preoccupied with what I am going to say. And I am not one content to be just a listener at a party. By the time I have contributed voluntarily—not counting the questions asked me—to the conversations across and down both sides of the speakers' long table, where I am sitting, and above the sound of a roomful of other women doing approximately the same thing, my voice is more closely akin to the Liberty Bell which is cracked, than to a silver bell which is not. When I have finished my stint, I long for people, talk, and, yes, food, of the scrambled egg and toast family. Anyone performing a piece is raised to his highest pitch in order to give out to the best of his ability what he has to give. It is hard to lower that pitch slowly.

I can understand, however, why a Sponsor Party prefers its celebration beforehand. The members have other things to do—families and dinner are waiting, or, if the "do" is at night, the men want to get home. They can't sleep on the train, or late next morning, like a lecturer. More important even, than these domestic influences, there is always the strong possibility that the visiting furnishing may turn out to be a complete dud. The organization, nevertheless, will at least have had a party, and before they found out about him. If he is a dud, certainly no one wants to continue with him after his allotted hour on the platform. Therefore, I accept the timing. I am, after all, the one person who should not question it, since I am the doubtful party. I could also accept the chicken patties were it not for the weeks of shredded and unleavened lettuce they cause to follow. But there is a kind of food which I find difficult to take.

Mr. Otis Skinner used to tell about the five-year-old daughter of an actor who accompanied her father one day to the Players Club for lunch, and was allowed to sit at its long table with those august members lunching there. The child was beautifully behaved and silent throughout the meal. But as she pushed her chair back and rose from the table, she obeyed the rule that a guest must make some conversational contribution to the social occasion. And hers was:

"There are a kind of dog that has two rows of buttons down his stummick."

I wish I could be as articulate and leave my hearers with as vivid an impression of the phenomenon I wish to describe. I only know that "there are a kind" of food throughout the country which I find difficult to identify or assimilate. I think I can trace its source. I think it comes from the homemakers pages in women's magazines. But the source material has been used only as a base on which to superimpose flights of individual fancy confusing to the eye and to the taste buds. At one time in my life, when I worked on a woman's magazine, I could identify almost any food novelty. A cluster of shredded carrots, beneath it a ball of cream cheese punctuated by bits of dates and a sliver of cranberry, all that surmounting a twirl of lettuce, with a toothpick at either side, and two below it—and I knew at a glance this was a Raggedy Ann Salad. But either my eye has lost its cunning or Raggedy Ann is to newer confections as Mary Pickford to Lauren Bacall. I do not say that I dislike the new medleys, but I am bewildered by them.

In the Raggedy Ann days an avocado was an "alligator pear" and it was usually cut in half, filled with French dressing and scooped out with a spoon. It was a salad and you could tell that because there was a leaf of lettuce underneath it. Not long ago I had at a Sponsor party lunch half an alligator pear filled with creamed chicken, covered with cheese, baked, and called, because I asked, "Avocado Dream," and it was an appetizer. A few weeks ago at another of these functions, I tossed off what in my simplicity I took to be a glass of tomato juice. That turned out to be a highly spiced, rum-flavored concoction with a faintly discernible tomato base, and blistering hot. When I delivered my lecture, my eyes were still streaming and my voice, the voice of Jimmy Durante.

A city in the Northwest will live in my memory forever. Every detail of the table decoration particularly is embedded in my mind because I concentrated on each of them, chattering hysterically about the charm of the appointments, in order to avoid looking down at the dish presented before me for the first course. I had never seen that concoction before and with all my heart I pray that I may never see it again. It was half a grapefruit with, floating in its center, four raw oysters. I like grapefruit, and raw oysters are among my favorite foods, but, unreasonably, I prefer to remove them myself from the shell. Removed by other hands and placed in that strange setting, they looked to me like eyes, and I had no inclination to scoop them up with a spoon. But I did, and though I do not remember the rest of the meal, at least I kept it.

A very short time after this triumph, I received at the kindly hand of hospitality a trouncing and an exposure of my own social inadequacy that has put me in my place on a lecture tour. And my place is, or ought to be, when lecturing and away from my own simple environment— the hotel room. On the day of my exposure, I lunched with the executive committee of the organization for which I was to speak in the afternoon. The group was made up of 15 women, all of them charming, and the lunch was at the house of the president. The house was charming too. We had lively talk about it in the living room while we drank tomato juice, and about our children, the cost of food, the difficulty of getting material these days that would stand up, and we pranced into the dining room at the call of lunch in fine humor. The table was beautifully decorated and I said so immediately, giddily pleased with myself for being aware of this, because when I was at college, I learned from experiments we made in psychology that I am not a visualizer. I remember the things that I hear at a party and the things I eat, but I do not usually carry home a picture of how the table looked. At this luncheon, however, I noticed the decorations and I commented. The hostess was pleased, too.

The first course was a thick soup covered in whipped cream. I knew then that my girdle and I were going to have trouble getting together again, and that I would have to coax it back with days of Ry-Krisp and lettuce. The next course looked to me like a birthday cake except that it carried no candles. I wondered nervously if I could have been daydreaming and had already eaten the first course. I was seated at the right of the hostess and the large white mound was presented to me first to penetrate. Not until I had maneuvered a slice of it onto my plate, did I discover that the fantasy was made up of paper thin layers of chicken salad sandwiches covered over with cream cheese. The salad which came around immediately to be eaten with this was an aspic swathed in mayonnaise. By this time the cream and other rich substances were making me drowsy, and in an after-a-heavy-meal torpor, I had the dreamy feeling, struggling through the summit of this meal, that I was climbing an alp by my teeth and unable to bite through to any-

thing firm beneath the snowdrifts. The dessert
was another drift—angelfood cake. The straw-
berries covering it had been crushed out of any
resistant texture into a pulp, and the whole was
topped by a crest of whipped cream. I had long
since given up any attempt at conversation. I had
not breath enough for it, but I munched my way
through what I felt must be the last drift and was
aware of the maid at my elbow again. She was
presenting to me a 25 pound cake of ice resting
on a silver tray and covered with long-stemmed
pink roses. The offering startled me immediately
out of my torpor. I had visibly reached an ice-
topped peak. But confronted with the sight, I
did not know what to do with it. I saw no instrument with which to hack off a piece to deposit
on my plate. In my childhood, one of my favorite
delicacies was a piece of ice sucked through a
washrag, but this seemed not the occasion for
that reminiscent treat. The next best thing would
be to press my forehead gratefully against it, but
it would be a little odd perhaps, I thought, if we
all did that one by one. I should, of course, have
asked my hostess what it was for, but I was addled
by the food which had preceded it, and by the
unconscionable time I felt I had spent staring at

it with, I was sure, the other guests regarding me. With prayerful gratitude for a sudden inspiration, I lifted a rose from the floating cake. The maid accepted this and moved her slithering bounty on to the next guest. To sit with a rose in my hand was not to be sufficiently responsive, I thought, and so, I smelled it vigorously and then waved it from its long stem toward my hostess.

"Sweet," I said, "perfectly sweet."

By this time, my neighbor, who had followed my pattern, had her nose in her rose too, and she thereupon copied my waving. The other guests caught on quickly, and by the time the maid had completed the circle to the hostess, we were all smiling, sniffing, waving and saying "Sweet."

The hostess smiled back, but more in pity than in praise, as she brushed aside the few remaining roses and drew her fingers delicately over the surface of the block of ice. She had thought up, herself, this elfin variation of the humdrum finger-bowl.

I took my coffee black.